guitar world

the guitarist's almanac

BY ALAN DI PERNA

HAL•LEONARD®

Library of Congress Cataloging-in-Publication Data:

Di Perna, Alan, 1953-
The guitarist's almanac / written by Alan di Perna.
p. cm.
ISBN 0-7935-7230-4. – ISBN 0-7935-6851-X (pbk. : library binding)
1. Guitar. I. Title.
ML 1015.G9D5 1997
787.87' 19—dc21 97-51796
CIP
MN

the guitarist's almanac

B Y ALAN DI PERNA

ISBN 0-7935-6851-X

HAL•LEONARD®
CORPORATION
7777 W. BLUEMOUND RD. P.O. BOX 13819 MILWAUKEE, WI 53213

Visit Hal Leonard Online at
www.halleonard.com

Table of contents

TEN MILESTONES IN THE DEVELOPMENT OF THE MODERN GUITAR

PETE TOWNSHEND

©Baron Wolman / Retna LTD.

the historical guitarist

No one is certain exactly when the first guitar appeared. All we know is that, sometime, someplace in sixteenth-century Europe, boom, there it was—this elegant, narrow-waisted beauty with a fretted fingerboard and a sonic character distinct from all the other stringed instruments.

"I think the guitar is one of the great great instruments of the last few hundred years. It's so expressive in its new, electric form. When you pick up a fairly modern, fine-tuned custom electric guitar and put it through a batch of modern electronics, you can make it do anything. I really love the way that the guitar is a product of the technological age."
...Pete Townshend

The guitar's portability and harmonic possibilities made it an ideal traveling companion for wandering minstrels, mountebanks, gypsies, courtly lovers, and other post-feudal hipsters. But at the same time, the guitar's sonorous tone earned it a place in the finest concert halls. The guitar has always been an instrument "of the people"—a popular instrument, that is. And because of its close links with popular music, the guitar has evolved at an incredible pace over the past 400 years, en route to becoming the ultimate rock machine it is today.

Here are some major milestones in that development:

1850s–'90s – Antonio de Torres Juardo develops the classical guitar.

1902 – Orville Gibson establishes the Gibson guitar company.

Circa 1930 – The birth of the electric guitar. Rickenbacker and Vivi-Tone produce some of the earliest commercial models.

Circa 1946 – At the prompting of guitarist Merle Travis, Paul Bigsby invents the Bigsby vibrato arm tailpiece.

1949 – The Fender Broadcaster is introduced. In 1951, the guitar was given a new name: the Fender Telecaster.

1952 – The Gibson Les Paul is introduced. Designed in collaboration with radio personality, guitarist, and recording pioneer Les Paul, the instrument was specifically designed as an upmarket alternative to the Fender Telecaster.

1966 – At the urging of Pete Townshend, guitarist for the Who, Jim Marshall builds the first 100-watt guitar amp and "stack."

1967 – The dawn of synthetic materials. Ovation introduces the first acoustic guitar with a body made from synthetic fibers, originally developed in the manufacture of helicopter blades. Synthetic materials would later be used in guitars and basses made by Modulus Graphite (introduced in 1977), Steinberger (introduced in 1979), and Parker Fly guitars (introduced in 1993).

1977 – Floyd Rose invents the locking-nut vibrato system that bears his name.

Circa 1980 – The guitar enters the digital era. The MXR DDL and Deltalab Effectron begin to take over from tape-based echo and seventies analog stomp boxes. The Yamaha SPX-90 (1984) brings the ability to produce multiple digital effects—hundreds of different guitar sounds in one box! The advent of guitar synthesis (1980) and MIDI (1983) gives guitarists access to a far-flung universe of sounds.

KNOW YOUR GUITAR PARTS

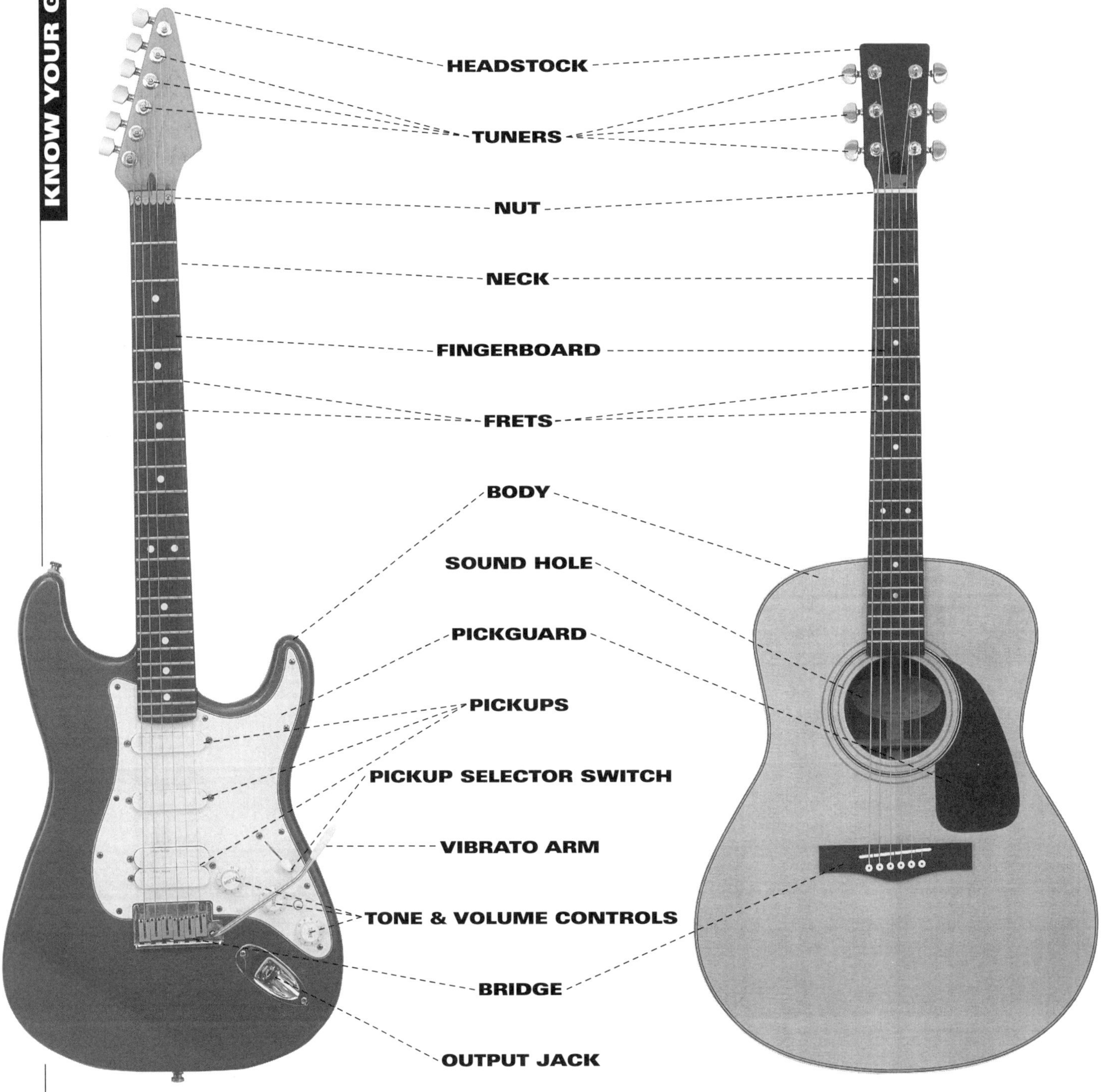

UNDERSTANDING HOW GUITAR EQUIPMENT WORKS

CARLOS SANTANA

© Jay Blakesberg / Retna LTD.

the informed guitarist

WHY GUITARS SOUND THE WAY THEY DO

"A note is like a rose. It can be closed or halfway open or all the way in bloom. You have to know when to hit that note the right way." ...Carlos Santana

Vibration, that's why. Each guitar string is like a cable stretched taut between two nodes: the bridge at one end of the guitar and the nut at the other. Each of these nodes is anchored in wood (generally). The bridge is attached to the body, and the nut is slotted into the neck. When a string is plucked, vibrations travel along the string and down the bridge and nut. The energy is transferred to the body and neck wood, which also start to vibrate. These vibrations then travel back up the neck and nut, modifying the way the string is vibrating.

It's like a mini-earthquake: a complex physical phenomenon with energy waves flowing in all directions, colliding, canceling, altering, and reinforcing one another. Out of this benign cataclysm comes the thing they call tone. This is true for electric guitars as well as acoustics. Pickups, amplifiers, and effects can only pick up, amplify, and affect the physical vibrations coming off the instrument itself.

So a guitar's tone is determined by the resonant properties of its parts—the way each of these parts reflects and absorbs vibrations from the strings. Let's look at some of the most important variables.

© Larry Busacca

JEFF BECK

HOLLOWBODY VS. SOLIDBODY

All acoustic guitars are hollowbodied instruments, with an open inner chamber. This resonant cavity turns the subtle vibrations of the guitar's top, back, and sides into bigger, louder soundwaves and sends them out the sound hole. **Flat-top** acoustic guitars traditionally have a large, centrally located sound hole and a full, warm sound like you hear in folk music, bluegrass, and other "unplugged" genres. **Archtop** guitars, as their name implies, have a curved top, traditionally with two *f*-holes located at either side of the strings. (They're called *f*-holes because they look like the letter "f" in script writing.) These ***f*-holes** are smaller and narrower than the big, round sound holes on flat-tops. This feature, occurring as it does on a curved wooden surface, generally gives archtop guitars a brighter, jazzier tone than flat-tops.

On higher-quality, more expensive hollowbody guitars, the top is made of solid wood—spruce, most commonly. Less expensive ones have laminated

"When I bought my first Rickenbacker [in 1965] and stuffed it with paper, I found I could actually produce feedback on harmonics, which was quite extraordinary. I found I could reproduce it live by moving the guitar in relation to the speakers." ...Pete Townshend

WHAT IS FEEDBACK?

Feedback is what happens when your pickups and speakers start to interact. Technically it's called a transduction loop. A transducer is something that converts one form of energy into another. Pickups convert string vibrations into electricity. Speakers convert electricity into vibrations (sound waves). Feedback occurs when vibrations from the speaker re-excite the strings. The pickup picks up these vibrations and converts them back into an electrical signal, sending the sound back through the amp and out the speakers again. If it's not interrupted (by muting the strings with your hand), the loop will cycle around continuously, growing louder and louder. This is why feedback seems to "swell" once it gets started. As the strings vibrate more and more energetically, the pitch of the feedback will begin to rise in harmonic intervals.

If you want to avoid feedback, don't stand in a position where your pickups are directly facing your speakers. If you want to induce feedback for creative purposes, do stand with your pickups directly facing your speakers. Manipulating feedback for musical purposes is an art form in itself. It takes a lot of practice and it's virtually impossible to master 100 percent. Which is part of the excitement.

tops—thin layers of wood glued together. Solid wood tops vibrate more uniformly than laminates and therefore produce better tone and resonance.

Hollowbody electric guitars are most commonly archtops with pickups attached. They generally produce a warmer tone than solidbody electrics (see below). They also tend to produce feedback much more readily than a solidbody. This can be either a blessing or a curse, depending on your musical outlook. Feedback can be hard to control at high volumes. Then again, that never stopped Ted Nugent from using his hollowbody Gibson Byrdland for the past thirty years or so. A favorite trick of rock guitarists who play hollowbodies is to stuff the inside of the body with paper or cloth. This helps to control feedback, but you still get that hollowbody tone.

These days, the overwhelming majority of electric guitars sold are solidbody instruments. The type of wood that the body is made of has a big impact on

"There's as much style and technique in the way William Reed [of the Jesus and Mary Chain] gets his feedback as there is in the way Eddie Van Halen does hammer-ons." ...producer Alan Moulder

the tone of the guitar. Heavier woods like ash, maple, and mahogany give the instrument more sustain and generally contribute more to the tone, because they vibrate more. Some players like this and others don't. The ones who don't generally go for a very lightweight wood like swamp ash or basswood. These vibrate less and therefore "interfere" with string vibration to a lesser degree. Light woods were very popular with shred metal players a little while back. Heavier woods are more "classic rock." A very nice medium-weight wood is alder, which was used to make many early-sixties Fender Strats and other models.

HOW NECKS AFFECT TONE

How is the neck joined to the body on your guitar? The neck joint is one factor that affects the overall sound of the instrument. There are three types of neck joints, each with its own characteristic tone:

1. **Glued-In:** The most traditional design, the glued-in neck joint employs a dovetail, or tongue-and-groove, joint. A groove is cut into the wood of the body where the neck is to be attached. And the heel of the neck is carved to include a wooden "tongue," which slides into the groove and is held in place by glue. This is the type of neck joint used in many Gibson and Gibson-style guitars, including the Les Paul. Because the body and neck are very tightly joined, they vibrate almost as a single piece of wood. Which tends to promote a healthy amount of sustain—a quality for which Les Pauls are duly famous.

2. **Bolt-On:** This is a modern convenience invented by Leo Fender in the late 1940s. The lower portion of the neck slides into a "pocket" carved in the body and is then secured by bolts. This kind of neck has less of a heel down at the bottom; so some players find it more comfortable. From a repair standpoint, it's a brilliant idea. If something bad happens to your neck, it's a very simple matter to unscrew it and bolt in a new one. You can be rocking again in less than an hour—a time frame that would be impossible if a glue-in neck needed replacement. Tonally, bolt-on necks make for less sustain than glue-ins. But the bolt-on design has a lot to do with crisp, clean Fender-style guitar sounds.

3. **Neck-through-body:** This idea became popular during the seventies. The neck and the central portion of the body are made from a single piece of wood. Two "wing pieces" are usually attached to either side to make up the rest of the body. The idea is that any rift or joint between the neck and body will inhibit the transfer of vibrations from body to neck and vice versa, thus sucking up a certain amount of sustain.

Of course, it's not only how the neck and body are joined that affects the tone of the guitar. The neck material also contributes a lot to the sound. Particularly the fingerboard material. Of the two most common woods used for electric guitar fingerboards, maple generally makes for a brighter sound than rosewood. A light-colored wood, maple is much harder than the darker, more porous rosewood. A Strat with a maple fingerboard, for example, will sound noticeably brighter than the very same guitar with a rosewood fingerboard.

SCALE LENGTH AND STRING GAUGE

Technically speaking, a guitar's scale length is twice the distance from the nut to the twelfth fret. If the guitar is properly set up for intonation, this will equal the distance between the nut and the bridge saddles on your guitar: the total expanse of vibrating string on the instrument. Depending on the guitar, this can be anywhere from 24 to 26 inches. These two inches of vibrating string make a small but noticeable difference in tone and in playability. Also, guitar strings come in different thicknesses, or gauges. Heavier strings put out more volume and sustain. But here, playability should also be taken into account. There's not much sense in struggling with strings thicker than telephone wires just for some barely discernible tonal advantage.

HARDWARE DOES ITS BIT

The materials used to make guitar hardware also have an impact on tone. This is especially true for the **nut** and the **bridge**—the two points that directly convey string vibration to the wooden parts of the guitar.

Brass hardware provides more sustain than steel, because brass is denser than steel. Steel is brighter sounding than graphite or traditional bone or modern "phony bone" synthetics. Even fret wire can make a difference. Big, thick, "jumbo" frets add a little more brightness and sustain. Installing a Floyd Rose system will alter the tone of a guitar fairly radically. Because the bridge "floats" on a pivot point, there's minimal contact between the bridge and the body, which tends to reduce sustain. But since Floyds are mainly used in shred metal—a style in which guitarists are mainly playing ultra-fast muted arpeggios—this is less of an issue than it might otherwise be.

THE MYSTERIOUS X FACTOR

While it's good to be aware of how different parts of a guitar affect its sound, there's no reason to become obsessive about it. A guitar is more than the sum total of its parts. The way in which all those different parts interact is a phenomenon too complex to reduce to a set of rules—like the "chemistry" that exists among a group of people in a room. This is why a cheap guitar can sometimes sound better than an expensive one.

By the same token, all the fancy replacement parts and hardware in the world won't turn a crappy-sounding guitar into a gem. Before investing in a proposition like that, a player might do better just to sell the guitar and buy a new one.

WHAT IS SUSTAIN?

Sustain, quite simply, is how long a string will continue to sound after it's been struck. This might seem a moot point, since very few pieces of music call for strings to ring out indefinitely. But sustain will also affect how long a note will stay big and fat before it starts to wimp out—or decay, to use the technical term. Sustain can also be enhanced electronically via stomp boxes or standing close enough to your amp that the guitar is just on the verge of feeding back.

Is a whole lot of sustain always a good thing? Not necessarily. It's great for certain styles of single-note lead playing and for big crashing power chords that ring out for several bars of a song. In other words, it's good when you want your guitar to behave like a continuously-bowed violin or a piano with the sustain pedal pressed down. But players doing more rhythmic, "choppy" styles—funk, for example—often find that too much sustain just makes things "mushy." They want their guitars to behave more like a conga drum—with a crisp, aggressive attack and not too much "ring."

"The more a guitar is exposed to music, the better it gets. Wood goes through a molecular change as it's exposed to the vibrations of music. I've always noticed that guitars I've taken on tour seem to sound better a year later." ...Joe Satriani

JOE SATRIANI

© Simon Meaker/ Retna LTD.

the informed guitarist

THE ELECTRIC PART OF GUITAR TONE

The job of pickups, amplifiers, and speakers is to take the physical vibrations from the guitar, turn them into electricity, and then turn the electricity into big soundwaves that can fill a room. In doing their respective jobs, pickups, amplifiers, and speakers all have a major impact on the overall guitar tone. Electric guitarists can also add effects devices to the signal chain to further enhance and modify tone.

PICKUP FLAVORS

Pickups convert string vibrations into an electrical signal. There are four types of electric guitar pickups, each with its own characteristic sound.

1. **Single-Coil.** Simplicity itself: some wire wrapped around a magnet. Produces a crisp sound with lots of high frequencies—a tone very much associated with Fender guitars. One drawback of single coils is that they tend to produce a lot of hum when they get near fluorescent lighting, stage lights, and even other band equipment. Which is why a clever fellow named Seth Lover invented the...

2. **Humbucker.** A humbucking pickup (to give it its full and proper name) consists of wire coiled around two magnets. The two coils cancel out hum. The down side is that they also cancel out a lot of high frequencies. As a result, humbuckers have a bass-heavy sonic character: what people often call a "fat" or "beefy" tone. It's a sound closely associated with Gibson solidbody electrics (which are generally equipped with humbuckers), and Les Pauls in particular.

3. **Active.** Active pickup systems, such as EMGs, work with a small preamplifier built right into the guitar. By tweaking EQ on the preamp, it's possible to get a wide array of tones: single coil-style, humbucking-style, and otherwise. The only hitch is that you have to remember to change the preamp batteries. If you don't, the pickups will produce no tone whatsoever.

4. **Lace Sensor.** An airport security device that detects fancy lingerie. No, not really. Invented by Don Lace, these little guys produce a single-coil style sound without the hum. They come stock on many new Fender guitars.

AMP FAMILIES

Amplifiers take the weak little electrical signal coming off the pickups and convert it into a more powerful signal that can drive speakers. The specific components and circuit designs used to accomplish this job have a profound effect on tone. **Tube amps** are generally considered to be tonally superior to **solid-state** (transistor) amps. Clean sounds seem warmer. Distorted sounds seem creamier. The tradeoff is that tube amps are more expensive, more fragile, weigh more, and require more maintenance than their solid-state counterparts.

Amps come in many shapes and sizes. But most belong to one of three families:

1. **Combos.** A combo amp provides everything that's needed to amplify an electric guitar, all in one, more-or-less compact package. You get the amp, preamp, speakers, and sometimes a spring reverb and/or tremolo unit thrown in for good measure. Combo amps generally have open-backed speaker cabinets, which is the single greatest sonic characteristic of the "combo amp sound." Sound emanates from the back of the speaker cabinet as well as the front. It produces a very full, open guitar sound; a tone that can "breathe."

2. **Stacks.** Amp "stacks" are central to the iconography of rock—towering monuments to testosterone-fueled riffsmanship. The amplification electronics are packaged in a separate box from the speakers. The amp "head" is stacked on top of the speaker cabinets (usually two). The speakers cabinets generally have closed backs, which makes for a tighter, "punchier" sound than an open back cabinet. The design is ideally suited to the heavily overdriven guitar tones that stacks are so great at producing.

3. **Racks.** A by-product of the fast-lane eighties, rack amplification systems are like expensive stereo systems optimized for guitar signals. There are generally separate preamp and power amp modules, typically running in stereo and driving either a pair of conventional guitar cabinets or tweaky, hi-fi, full-range, closed-back speaker enclosures with separate woofers, tweeters, and (sometimes) midrange speakers. Plus there's usually an executive suite of digital effects processors. Everything but a mini bar! (And occasionally even that.) Rack systems are highly versatile. They can produce good combo- and stack-style tones, plus a universe of deep textures. But they are best in the hands of tech-oriented guitarists who aren't intimidated by a skyscraper of flashing LED's (light-emitting diodes) or equipment with software sub menus.

A WORD ABOUT SPEAKERS

The quality and size of the speakers used in an amp rig both have an impact on the overall guitar sound. Ten-inch and twelve-inch speakers are most commonly used in guitar amps. Ten-inchers have a tighter, brighter, punchier sound than twelves. The sound of four tens in an open-backed Fender Bassman cabinet is the tone that launched rock and roll—the quintessential "brown tone." Twelve-inchers have a slightly "flappier" but beefier tone. A twelve-inch speaker has a little more surface area than a ten. Because there's more material to "push," the speaker cone of the twelve moves a little slower. It's more of a "bruiser." Four twelves in a closed-back Marshall-style cabinet produce the definitive hard rock/heavy metal tone. For an even slabbier sound, some thrash metal players use fifteen-inchers, a speaker dimension what was formerly the domain of bassists. Factors that determine the quality of a speaker include the size of its magnet and the weight, flexibility, and overall quality of the material used in the speaker cone.

THE THREE EFFECTS FOOD GROUPS

Effects can be the icing on the cake or the main course of a good guitar sound. Guitar effects devices take the form of affordable, easy to use "stomp boxes" or more sophisticated rack mount units. Guitar effects can be produced by either analog or digital circuitry. Any way you choose it, there are three families of effects:

1. **Gain-Related Effects:** distortion/overdrive/fuzz, compressor/limiters, noise gates, EQ.

   Distortion happens when you increase the power (gain) of the guitar signal so it overdrives the amp. This can be done just by turning the amp up real loud. But by adding a distortion device to your rig, you can switch between distorted and clean sounds without having to take your hands off the guitar and fiddle with amp knobs.

   Most modern distortion pedals come with built-in **compression.** Compression is an effect that helps you tailor distortion. It's like an amplifier with a brain. It boosts the quiet parts of your signal and cuts back the loudest bits. This produces a more uniform guitar signal that makes for smoother distortion and added sustain.

   A **limiter** is very similar to a compressor, except that it only squashes the top part of the signal. You set a threshold and the limiter says, "Okay, I'm not going to let the signal get any louder than this. If anything louder than this comes along, I'm gonna turn it down." Everything below the threshold is remains unaffected.

A **noise gate** isn't really an effect—it doesn't make a wild sound or anything. But it becomes a necessity if you're using a lot of distortion and other effects that add noise to your rig. A noise gate is like an upside-down limiter. It cuts all volume when nothing's being played, so no hissy noise is heard. Then as soon as you play a note, the gate "opens up" letting the sound through.

Equalization, or **EQ,** lets you increase the volume of very specific frequencies. It's like a very fancy set of tone controls. A graphic EQ slices the whole frequency spectrum up into bands, on which you can cut or boost volume. A parametric EQ lets you tune in on specific frequencies and then cut or boost them.

2. **Time-Domain Effects:** chorus, flanging, phasing, delay, echo, reverb.

All these effects (except for phasing) work by doubling your guitar signal and then playing back that double image a little bit after the main signal is sounded. **Flanging** and **chorus** involve "double images" that follow the main signal by just a few milliseconds. Technically speaking, **phasing** uses filters rather than a time delay to produce its characteristic sound. But that sound very much belongs to the same family as flanging and chorus. They're all effects that "fatten" the sound by creating a continuously varying frequency shift.

If you keep increasing the time interval between the main signal and its double, eventually the double will become a separate, audible event. When that happens, we've entered the domain of **delay**—rockabilly slapback, spacey **echo,** all that stuff. Delay devices let you vary the number of times a signal repeats. And multitap delays allow you to set up a number of different repeat times.

Reverb is just a highly sophisticated version of this: ghost images of the main signal that repeat at many different time intervals and volume levels, simulating the way sound bounces around a room.

3. **Pitch shifting.**

A **pitch shifter** (or **Harmonizer,** to use a trademarked name) also creates a double image of the main signal. But instead of delaying the playback time of this double image, a pitch shifter transposes its pitch. "Intelligent" pitch shifters can follow a chord progression, changing the transposed pitches accordingly to create "instant Outlaws" guitar arrangements.

How to Hook Up Effects: Tales of the Chain Gang

For all the good they do in the world, effects can also add unwanted noise to your setup. So one goal in hooking up multiple effects is to do so in a way that minimizes noise. From this standpoint, the golden rule is to place gain-based effects (like distortion) before time-based effects (like chorus or reverb) in the signal chain. This way, the gain-based stuff won't be boosting the noise from flangers, echoes, reverbs, etc. This rule holds true whether you're connecting stomp boxes in a row or programming a chain of effects in a digital multi-effects rack unit.

Theoretically, the best place to connect a row of effects, or a single multi-effects unit, is between the preamp and power amp sections of your amplifier. And this is exactly where an effects loop on an amp will position them. One advantage here is that the effects are placed after the initial gain stage (the preamp). Also, when the effects aren't being used, they can be switched completely out of the signal path—"out of the loop" as "power guy" businessmen like to say. Without an effects loop, the signal would still have to pass through the effects unit, which is placed in bypass mode when the effect is not in use. Even in bypass mode, however, the effects device will still "color" the sound in some (probably undesirable) way.

Gain matching is a key concept to understand when connecting devices to an effects loop. It's a very simple concept: just make sure that the signal level coming out of the preamp (out of the effects send jack) matches the level that the effects unit is set up to receive. Most rack effects have a switch that lets you select between –20 dB (guitar level) and +4 dB (line level). You need to select line level for use with an effects loop. (The –20 is for plugging

"I much prefer stomp boxes to rack effects. You step on a pedal and you have your sound. It's easy. And I want it to be easy. When I've gotta do something on the spur of the moment, I don't want to have to start dialing up numbers on a computer. When you're in the heat of the moment and it's really pumping, do you want to get out a slide rule?" ...Dave Navarro

a guitar directly into the effect device.) Some effects units are marked simply "instrument" and "line." Along with this selector, most units also give you a knob and an LED marked "input level." Play your guitar into the rig, watch the LED, and tweak the knob till you've got a good strong signal that goes "into the red" on momentary peaks only. This fine tuning is necessary because different guitars will put a different level of signal into the amp.

You also need to adjust the level of the signal as it leaves the effects unit and goes back into the amp. Most rack effects give you an output level knob for doing this. The signal should be hot enough to drive the power stage of the amp without overloading it. On better amps, the effects loop input and output will also have knobs for tweaking level. Using them, you can tweeze your amp rig like a fine-tuned engine—so that it's running neither too hot nor too cold.

Why is gain matching important? If you put too "hot" a signal into the effects unit, it will distort. If you put too wimpy a signal into it, you'll have a bad signal-to-noise ratio. In other words, the unit will run noisily.

Of course, you don't have to connect your effects to an effects loop at all. For instance, many guitarists like to place distortion/overdrive boxes directly between the guitar and amp (i.e., before the preamp). This enables them to "hit the front end" with a lot of gain, which overloads the preamp, producing a nice, grungy kind of distortion. They're willing to live with a little extra noise to achieve this particular tone. So in the final analysis, the best way to hook up effects is the way that sounds best to you. It's hard to get an original sound if you're always following rules. Indeed, many of the wild, innovative tones employed by modern rock guitarists were achieved by using effects in ways that would horrify their guitar-playing dads.

BUDDY GUY

© David Redfern / Retna LTD.

the practical guitarist

BASIC STUFF

THE CORRECT WAY TO PUT ON STRINGS:

Unless you employ a full time guitar roadie, you'll have to change your own guitar strings. Broken strings need to be replaced, obviously. And in time, all strings get old and cruddy. When that happens, they no longer sound nice and bright like they did when they were new. So they've gotta be changed too. The thing is, it must be done the right way. If the strings aren't properly attached to the tuning machine capstans, you'll probably have problems with the guitar going out of tune.

SLASH

© Ian Tilton / Retna LTD.

Here's the correct way to attach strings to standard capstans on a traditional three-on-a-side machine head:

1. Turn the tuning peg until the capstan hole is in line with the nut slots.
2. Pass the string through the capstan hole, leaving some slack. (You want to leave enough slack for the string to wrap around the capstan two or three times. If there are any more wraps than this, there will be tuning problems. After a while, you'll get a sense for how much slack to leave for each string.)
3. Wrap the string around the capstan, underneath itself. Wrap it clockwise for the three bass strings and counterclockwise for the three treble strings. After wrapping it under, pull it upwards. This should put a good right-angle bend in the string that will keep it from slipping.
4. Tighten the tuning peg. On the second turn, the string should start to wrap around the capstan underneath itself. You may find it necessary to guide the string with your free hand while turning the peg.

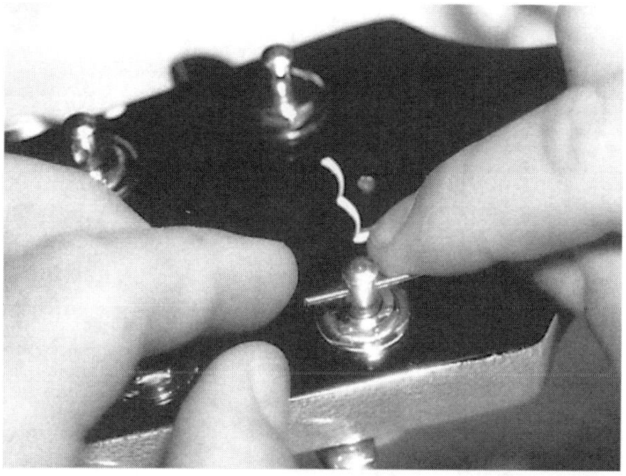

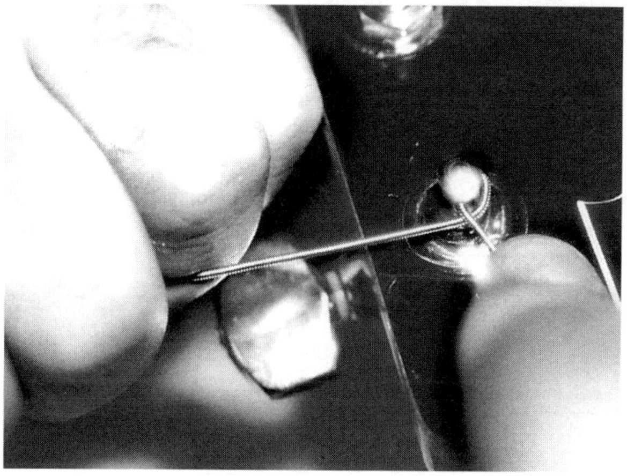

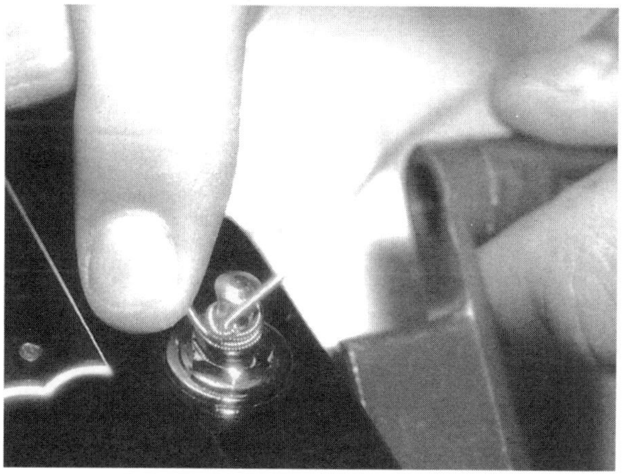

And that's it. If your guitar has all six tuning pegs on one side of the machine head, wrap all the strings counterclockwise around the capstan when you do step 3 above. (Clockwise for left-handed, six-on-a-side guitars.)

Once you've brought the string up to pitch, play some extreme note bends on it. Or slip your finger under the string, pull it up away from the fret board, then release it and let it snap back into place. If the string has gone out of tune, bring it back up to pitch. Doing this once or twice will tighten the string wrap around the capstan. When you're finished, there should be no overlaps and no gaps between the wraps.

If tuning problems persist—or if the procedure above seems too much like some sadistic nautical initiation rite—don't despair. Modern technology has given rise to several excellent brands of locking capstans that secure the strings via screws and other foolproof mechanical marvels.

"I went to Africa in 1970 and walked around the marketplace. I saw people playing the guitar. When they'd break a string, I swear to you, they'd tie a knot in it and use it again, because they didn't have any way to get a new one. I used to do it too when I was young. The string won't slip one bit if you know how to tie the knot right. Someone used to tease me about that—That's how you picked up a little speed, jumping over the knots!" ...Buddy Guy

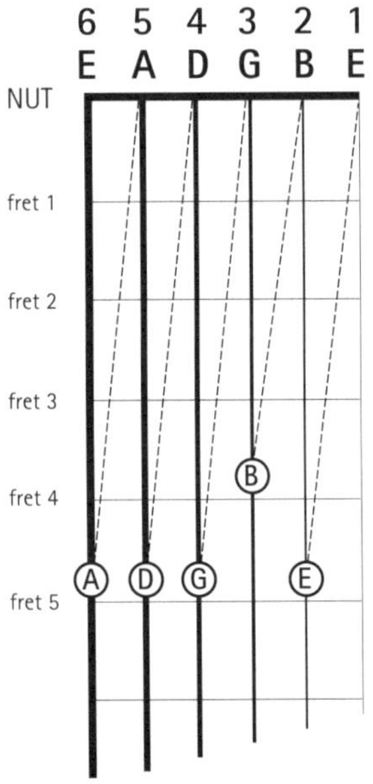

HOW GUITAR STRINGS ARE NUMBERED

They're numbered from the skinniest string to the fattest.

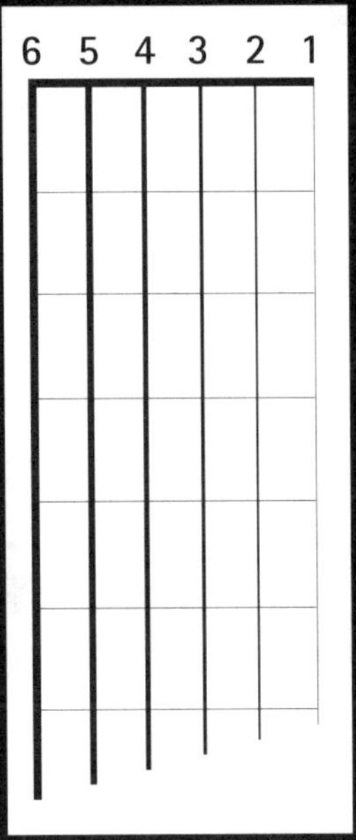

HOW TO TUNE YOUR GUITAR (STANDARD TUNING)

The six open strings of the guitar are tuned (from the low string to the high) E, A, D, G, B, E. There's an old phrase to help guitarists remember these intervals: Every Alligator Digs Great Big Elephants. This phrase has the virtue of being so stupid that it's almost impossible to forget.

You can tune a guitar by finding these notes on a piano or other instrument and turning the guitar's tuning keys till the pitches match. Alternately, you can use an electronic tuner, which will sound the pitches for you and also provide a VU meter, LED display, or some other visual aid to let you know when you've tuned the string to the correct pitch.

But once you've got one guitar string in tune, you can tune all the others relative to that one, without any outside tonal reference. Here's the easiest and most common method for doing this:

1. Get the low E (sixth) string in tune. You can accomplish this using any of the methods mentioned above. Or by playing a record that you know is in the key of E.
2. Find the fifth fret on the E string, put your finger there, play the resulting note. You will now be playing an A—the note you need to tune the next string over (the fifth string). Turn the fifth string tuning peg until the pitch of the open fifth string matches that of the low E string played at the fifth fret.
3. Repeat this procedure for the fourth and third (D and G) strings.

   Playing the fifth string at the fifth fret gives you a D—the note you need to tune the fourth string.

   Playing the fourth string at the fifth fret gives you a G—the note you need to tune the third string.
4. Now play the third string at the fourth fret. This gives you a B—the note you need to tune the second string.
5. Play the second string at the fifth fret. This gives you an E, the note you need to tune the first string.

INTERMEDIATE STUFF

HOW TO SET UP YOUR GUITAR

"Setting up" a guitar means adjusting two things: the guitar's action and its intonation. These operations can be performed by a guitar shop for a nominal fee. But if you're the kind of person who can use hand tools without inflicting bodily harm on yourself or others, you could try doing it yourself. When you do a setup, you adjust the action first, then the intonation.

*"When Van Halen first started playing clubs I had this Les Paul Junior that just wouldn't stay in tune. In between songs I'd say, 'Wait a minute, I gotta tune.' And the other guys in the band would say, 'F*** tuning, just play!' My brother Alex [Van Halen's drummer] and I would get into fights about it all the time. We used to play this place called Gazarri's on Sunset Strip where we didn't have a dressing room or anyplace to tune. So I'd have to tune right on stage, and Alex hated that, 'cause he thought it was so unprofessional. And rightly so, but at the same time, I had to tune, right?" ...Edward Van Halen*

SETTING THE ACTION

A guitar's action is determined, quite simply, by how high the strings are off the fretboard. This height always increases as you move up the neck, away from the headstock. If the strings are too high, the guitar will be uncomfortable to play. If they're too low, the strings will rattle against the frets, a phenomenon known as **fret buzz**. You want to set the action somewhere between these two extremes. Exactly where is a matter of personal preference, which is one reason why it's good for players to do this adjustment themselves. Four things govern a guitar's action: (1) how the neck is bowed, (2) the height of the nut slots, (3) the angle of the neck, and (4) the height of the bridge saddles.

1. Start by checking the **neck bow**. Ideally, you want the neck to be very slightly curved, or bowed, away from the strings. You can measure this by using the low E string as a straight edge. Holding the guitar in playing position, on a table, or on your lap, press the low E string down to the fretboard at the first fret. With one finger of your other hand, press the same string down at the twelfth fret. Examine the area around the middle (fifth through eighth) frets and observe how much of a gap there is between the string and the frets. The gap should be somewhere between 1/64 and 2/64 (1/32) of an inch. (You can verify these measurements by using a ruler.)

   If the amount of neck bow seems all right, you can move on to step 2 below. If there's a huge gap between the strings and the fretboard, the neck may be irreparably warped. Which is real bad news, because you'll

"[Folksinging legend] Pete Seeger is a wonderful, fantastic human being—'America's Tuning Fork,' they called him at one time. I learned guitar off the Pete Seeger Guitar Teacher record. That was the first instruction I ever had. The first track taught you how to tune it. That was pretty important." ...David Gilmour

have to get a new neck. If, however, the gap is a little bigger or smaller than what you'd like, you can correct this using the guitar's **truss rod**. The truss rod is a slightly curved metal shaft that's embedded in the neck.

When you tighten the rod, you're straightening the neck (i.e., creating less neck bow). When you loosen the rod, you increase the amount of neck bow. Truss rod adjusters are located either in the headstock or at the base of a fingerboard. They're operated by means of a screw, nut, or hex socket fitted into the rod. So to do this job, you'll need the appropriate tool (screwdriver, socket wrench, or hex [Allen] key). On most guitars, you turn the adjuster clockwise to tighten it (for less bow) and counterclockwise to loosen it. Most importantly, *never turn the rod too much!* Give it half a turn at most. Then wait. Because wood is cellular, organic matter, it will take a while to "settle in" around the new truss rod position. Wait half an hour or more. Then check the neck. Is the neck bow perfect now? Good. Leave the truss rod alone. If not, give it another small turn (no more than half a turn, remember?) and wait another half hour.

2. Now turn your attention to the nut. The **nut slots** have to be higher than the first fret. Otherwise, when you play notes down low on the neck, there'll be a sitar-like buzzing—which may sound cool if want to do a Ravi Shankar imitation, but isn't good for much else. Conversely, the nut slots shouldn't be too much higher than the first fret, or playing discomfort will set in and the intonation (see below) could get funny.

   So here's the test for proper nut slot height. Press down the low E string at the third fret. Then look at the distance between the string and the first fret.

   There should be some space there, even if it's only about as thick as a dog hair. Taking your finger and poking the string at the first fret, while still holding it down at the third, will help you determine this. If there's just a small space like this, the nut's okay and you can go on to steps 3 and 4 below.

   But if the string is resting directly on the first fret, then the nut slot is too low. There are two ways to remedy this: a brand new nut, or a thin wooden strip (called a **shim**) placed beneath the existing nut to raise the slot height. Both options are jobs that should only be done by someone experienced at guitar repair work.

   But what if the string is too high off the first fret when you test it? Then the nut slots are too high. The solution here is to file the slots down lower. This is another job that you should probably not try to do yourself. First of all, you have to have the right kind of file. Even then, if you go just a *weensy* bit too far with the file, you'll make the slot too deep and the nut will be ruined. Also, you have to file all six slots down exactly the same amount, or else the guitar will never feel right when you play it. Still, you can try doing it yourself, as long as you're willing and able to have a guitar shop cut a new nut for you (which will cost more than having a shop file the slots on the existing nut).

3. (Optional) On guitars with bolt-on necks, a shim can also be used to change the **neck angle**. This is an option if there's too much string height up at the high end of the fretboard, but the action is perfect down at the low end of the fretboard and the neck bow is just fine. To shim a bolt-on neck, you remove the strings, unbolt the neck, and place a thin, wedge-shaped piece of wood—a shim—in the inside angle of the slot where the neck sits. Which means you must have the tools and skill to cut out a small wedge-shaped piece of wood to pretty close tolerances.

   You should only shim the neck as a last resort—if you can't get the results you want by adjusting the truss rod, nut slot height, and bridge height (see below).

4. The last step in setting a guitar's action is to adjust the height of the **bridge saddles**. On many electric guitars, the height of each individual saddle can be adjusted. On Fenders, for example, each saddle sits on two "legs" that are actually Allen screws that pass through the saddle. Turning the screws makes the "legs" longer or shorter, thus changing the saddle height. On other bridges—including Gibson Tune-O-Matics and some Floyd Roses—individual saddle heights are not adjustable. Instead, the saddles are attached to a horizontal bridge piece that rests on two vertical posts. You can adjust the height of the posts, which means you can slant the bridge. The general procedure is to start by adjusting the bass side. You may find it a good idea to set the action a little higher for the bass strings than for the treble strings. Bass strings have more **excursion**—they move further than the skinny little treble strings when they vibrate. So they're more likely to slap against the frets and buzz.

On acoustic guitars, the bridge saddle is generally a single piece of bone (or bonelike material) with six small grooves to hold the strings in place. You lower an acoustic guitar saddle by taking it out of its slot in the bridge and sanding some material off the bottom. You raise it by placing a shim beneath it in its slot.

SETTING THE INTONATION

After the action has been fully adjusted, the next part of setting up a guitar is to check the intonation and adjust it if necessary. Setting the **intonation** involves fine-tuning the length of each string so that the guitar "frets true"—i.e., notes are at their correct pitches—all up and down the neck.

Here's the test: Play a harmonic at the twelfth fret of each string (see page 32: "How to Play Harmonics"). Then fret the note at the twelfth fret. Compare the two pitches. Is the fretted note sharp or flat as compared with the harmonic? (You can use an electronic tuner to make certain.) If so, then the intonation for that string needs to be adjusted. Each string needs to be tested in this manner. One string can be perfectly intonated and the one right next to it can be off.

Intonation is set by moving the bridge saddles forward or backward. On some old archtops, the whole bridge has to be moved, but on most electric guitars, each saddle is individually adjustable for intonation. An ordinary screwdriver is generally all that's needed for this. (Floyd Rose bridges require a 2.5 mm Allen wrench.) You also need a really good electronic tuner. Most pros recommend a strobe tuner. The less expensive VU meter tuners are not quite sensitive enough.

The procedure is fairly simple. You just move the saddles and repeat the harmonics test (using the tuner) until you get the intonation right. If the fretted note is sharper than the harmonic, move the saddle away from the neck. If the fretted note is flatter than the harmonic, move the saddle toward the neck. Owing to laws of physics too abstruse to discuss here, even the finest guitar in the world won't be perfectly intonated at every single fret. The procedure is a bit harder with Floyd Rose systems, because you have to detune the string each time you move the saddle.

Once you've adjusted the action and fine-tuned the intonation of each string, voilà, your guitar is completely set up. By this point, your next question is most likely...

Geez, how often do I have to go through all this?

If you live in a cold climate like the American Northeast or Midwest, you should check the action and intonation on your guitar twice a year: once after it gets real cold and once after it gets real hot. Since wood is organic matter, it reacts to changes in temperature and humidity. Cold contracts it, heat expands it. Humidity bloats it. The guitar may not have to be re-set up every time you test it. Or maybe the bridge saddles will just need to be tweaked a little. Guitars tend to need less adjusting in more hospitable climes. So if you loathe hand tools and can't find a good repair shop, you might consider moving to southern California.

ADJUSTING PICKUP HEIGHT

After a setup, or even a disappointing gig, you might feel inclined to change the height of your pickups. Positioning the pickup closer to the string will increase volume and alter the tone in a manner you might find agreeable. Only be careful not to position pickups too close to the strings, or you'll experience a phenomenon called **string drag**. This occurs when the pickup's magnetic field arrests string vibration, which will reduce sustain and make the string seem "dead." If you experience this kind of thing, even with brand new strings, you might take a look at how close your pickups are to the strings.

The actual procedure for adjusting pickup height is very easy. You'll find two screws at either side of the pickup. Just get a screwdriver and commence cranking. Clockwise to raise, counterclockwise to lower is the general rule. But you'll see the pickup moving; it'll be obvious. You'll be able to raise the treble side of the pickup higher than the bass side without experiencing string drag. This is because thinner strings have less excursion than fat ones. They don't travel as far so they don't get caught up in the pickup's magnetic field. Raising the treble side of the pickup is particularly helpful with Strats, which have a tendency to "wimp out" on the high strings.

So much for owner maintenance procedures. Now we move to...

THINGS YOU SHOULDN'T DO TO YOUR GUITAR (UNLESS YOU'RE A LUTHIER)

Fret jobs are best left to the pros. With time, frets wear down and start to develop "nicks" in areas where the strings vibrate most vigorously. If this goes on too long, the frets have to be taken out, new fret wire inserted, and the new frets filed and buffed to perfection. If caught in time, fret nicks can sometimes be remedied by a simple **grind and polish**—another service your friendly guitar shop will provide—without having to replace the fret wire.

As a general rule, a professional guitar repair person should be called in to do *any job that requires cutting a hole in the guitar.*

"Most of my repairs are hotel room repairs, done with screwdrivers and hammers. So my bass shows the results of my craftsmanship: It's pretty much a wreck." ...Billy Sheehan

This includes routing cavities for new pickups, installing new tuning machines, and installing a new bridge, such as a Floyd Rose. And, as mentioned earlier, cutting a new nut is a delicate operation that should be performed by a *bona fide* guitar doctor.

PREVENTATIVE MAINTENANCE: YOUR GUITAR'S FOUR BIGGEST ENEMIES

The best way to keep your guitar out of the shop is to treat it right in the first place. That means protecting it from things that might hurt it. There are four forces of nature that are particularly nasty to guitars and other string instruments:

1. **Temperature.** Your guitar is nearly as sensitive to heat and cold as you are. Maybe even more so. Too much cold can make a fretboard crack—particularly an ebony one. Excesses of temperature can warp a guitar neck permanently. From times immemorial guitar sages have counseled us: Never leave your guitar anyplace where you wouldn't be comfortable spending the night. Like car trunks and garages in the dead of winter. Or up on a luggage rack while driving across the Arizona desert when it's 124 degrees outside. A good guitar case can help keep an instrument at a reasonable temperature for a trek across town on a cold or hot day. But it can't protect your guitar from extremes like these. Be careful at outdoor shows too. Remember that the earth revolves on its axis, so a guitar left in the shade could be exposed to blazing sun an hour later. Also, if your guitar has been for a trip outside, try to let it get back to room temperature before you play. Otherwise you may find you have a problem keeping it in tune as the wood shakes off the effects of inclement climate.

2. **Moisture** (humidity, perspiration, and other vile fluids). Wood is pretty porous stuff. It tends to absorb moisture from the air. This makes the wood swell, which tends to throw intonation and action off kilter. So keep guitars indoors on rainy days and never park one by a pool. Guitars are lousy swimmers.

   Then there's the moisture produced by human sweat glands, which can be pretty nasty stuff—full of corrosives that eat away guitar strings and nice lacquer finishes. Which is why you should wipe your guitar neck after you play. You might also wipe off parts of the guitar that come into contact with bare skin, like the upper bout of the guitar body where the forearm rests, or, if you're in the Red Hot Chili Peppers or any other shirtless act, the entire back of the guitar. Yes, it's hard to remember to wipe your guitar off every time you play it. One way of prodding your memory is to keep a cotton T-shirt or other cloth in your guitar case or draped around your guitar stand. Only do remember to wash the T-shirt periodically.

BILLY SHEEHAN

© Jeff Tisman / Retna LTD.

As bad as moisture is, a lack of it can be even worse. Rosewood fingerboards have a tendency to dry out, particularly in arid climates such as the American Southwest. When a fingerboard dries out, it can become pitted or even cracked. So it's a good idea to lubricate rosewood fretboards with a few drops of a good lemon oil furniture polish a few times a year. Do it when you change strings and the fret-board's all naked anyway. You just need a drop or so between frets. Spread it around with a clean cotton cloth (not the one you've been mopping up sweat with!). Let the oil soak in a few seconds, then wipe away the excess. This exercise will also help deal with our next offender...

3. **Dirt.** Those tiny particles of grit, they're everywhere! Dirt can cause tuning problems. It gets into nut slots. Then when you bend a note, accumulated grit prevents the string from sliding back into place. The same thing happens when dirt gets into the moving parts of a whammy bar system. And when those tiny airborne scuzzballs get into tone and volume controls, they make 'em crackle and crap out.

   Guitars that earn their living in bars and other smoke-filled rooms are particularly vulnerable to microscopic grit. So are guitars that are kept on display, hanging on walls or standing on stands but rarely taken up and played. So don't forget to dust.

4. **Gravity.** Nothing's worse for a guitar than falling down. Tuning pegs get bent, wood splits, and all those precision adjustments you made when setting up your guitar get thrown out of whack. Never leave a guitar leaning up against a wall. The absolute worst thing to do is lean it with the strings facing the wall (i.e., with the back of the instrument facing into the room). The neck is in high danger of snapping right off the body—particularly if someone stumbles into the guitar.

How to Play Harmonics

Here's a cosmic fact: Every note is actually composed of several notes, or pitches. These pitches are all mathematically related to one another in what's called a harmonic series. Thus, they're called harmonics (or overtones, or partials). The most prominent member of the harmonic series is called the fundamental, a.k.a. the first harmonic. It's the pitch that enables us to say, "Oh, that's an E," or whatever note it may happen to be.

But also contained within that note is its second harmonic, which is an octave higher than the fundamental, its third harmonic, which is an octave and a fifth higher than the fundamental, its fourth harmonic, which is two octaves above the fundamental, its fifth harmonic, which is a major third above that, its sixth harmonic, which is a minor third above that, and so on. The harmonics keep going up until you get into pitches beyond the range of human hearing: the so-called dog harmonics (dogs being able to hear higher pitches than humans). On any given instrument, some harmonics will be slightly more or less prominent than others. Which is why no two instruments ever sound quite the same.

In guitar playing, there are a few techniques for sounding a single harmonic and suppressing all others. This is easiest to do with open-string notes (as opposed to fretted ones). This is called playing a natural harmonic. Here's the procedure:

Find the twelfth fret of your guitar. Place a left-hand finger over one of the strings as if you were going to play a note at the twelfth fret. Only don't press the note all the way down. Instead, just hold your finger lightly on the string. (Hint: Place your finger directly over the fret, not behind it.) Then pluck the string with your guitar pick or a finger of your right hand. As soon as the note begins to sound, lift your left-hand finger off the string. You should hear a ringing tone an octave higher than the open string (the fundamental). This is the second harmonic.

You can do the same thing on almost any fret, but certain ones will ring out more readily than others. Playing an open-string harmonic at the seventh fret gives you the third harmonic—a high fifth. Curiously enough, you'll get the exact same pitch if you play a harmonic at the nineteenth fret on the same string. It's all mathematics, actually. The seventh fret is one third the total length of the string from the nut. And the nineteenth fret is one third the total length of the string from the bridge—which comes to the same thing, harmonically speaking. In both cases the exact same lengths of string are vibrating.

Playing an open-string harmonic at the fifth fret will produce an even higher octave (the fourth harmonic). The fourth or ninth fret yields a high major third (fifth harmonic). Open-string harmonics are useful for checking the intonation and tuning of your guitar and can also be put to musical use. Listen to Jimi Hendrix's "Little Wing," for example, and you'll hear him playing with harmonics and the tremolo arm. One thing he does on that song—and it's actually a very easy technique—is place a finger lightly across an entire fret and play the harmonics on all six strings. Classic rock buffs will also recognize this sound from the intro to "Roundabout" by Yes.

But what if you want to play a harmonic of a note other than E, A, D, G, B, or E (i.e., the open-string notes)? The technique for that is a little trickier. First, fret the note that you want to be the fundamental in the usual way, using a left-hand finger. To play the second harmonic of that fundamental, go up twelve frets higher than the fretted note. Place the first finger of your right hand lightly over that fret and pluck the string with the thumb of the same hand, or with a pick grasped between the thumb and second finger. To play the third harmonic, do the same technique seven frets above the note being played by the left hand. For the fourth harmonic, do it five frets above the note being played by the left hand, and so on.

Another approach—an alternative to doing the two-finger drill with your right hand—is just to give the string a short, sharp tap with the first or second finger of the right hand at the fret where you want to play a harmonic. Warning: If you overuse this technique, your friends will start to call you Yngwie.

© Michael Putland / Retna LTD.

FRANK ZAPPA

the literate guitarist

Q: How do you get a rock guitarist to turn down?
A: Put some sheet music in front of him. ...an old joke

Actually, that joke hit closer to home during the fifties, sixties, and seventies. Back then, most rock guitarists, including the greats, were self-taught and communicated their musical ideas to one another via a few simple chord charts and the "show and tell" method. This is a completely valid approach—the oral tradition—and is still in wide use today. But the eighties also saw the rise of formal instruction in rock music. Schools sprang up, instructional videos came out, book publishers and guitar magazines began printing accurate transcriptions of popular rock songs.

Currently, there are three methods in use for representing guitar music visually: chord diagrams, tablature, and conventional music notation.

CHORD DIAGRAMS

Chords are what songs are made of. A songwriter devises a series of them—known as a chord progression—which defines the harmonic structure of a song—the underpinning that supports the vocal melody and instrumental solos. Every guitar chord that exists can be represented by a chord diagram: a little picture of a portion of the guitar neck, showing the strings, frets, and finger placement:

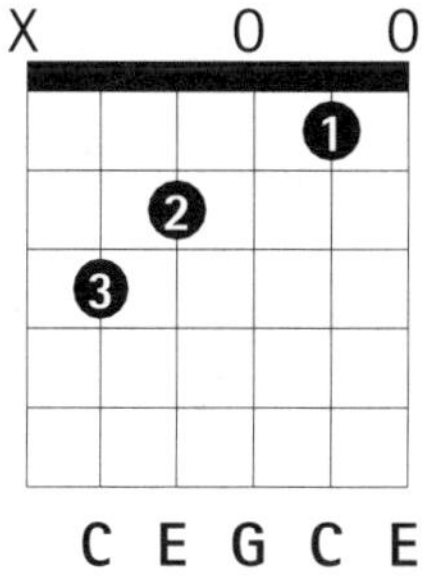

- The solid bar on top represents the nut.
- Vertical lines indicate the strings, from (left to right) the fattest (sixth) to the skinniest (first).
- Horizontal lines represent the frets.
- Filled-in circles show where to place the fingers.
- Numerals within the filled-in circles indicate which finger to use to play that note. (See fingering chart below.)
- An "o" placed over a string indicates that the string should be played "open".
- An "x" over a string means the string should not be played.
- A fret number (consisting of a number and the abbreviation "fr") is used to indicate the position of chords played higher up on the fretboard than the first four frets. (Roman numerals, rather than arabic, are sometimes used for this purpose.)
- A curved line is often used to indicate situations in which one finger holds down two or more strings simultaneously. This is called a **barre**.

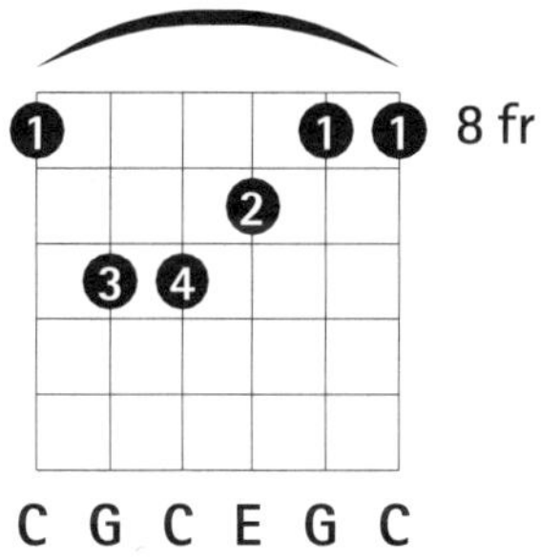

LEFT-HAND FINGER NUMBERS

The thumb is not numbered. The other four fingers are as shown.

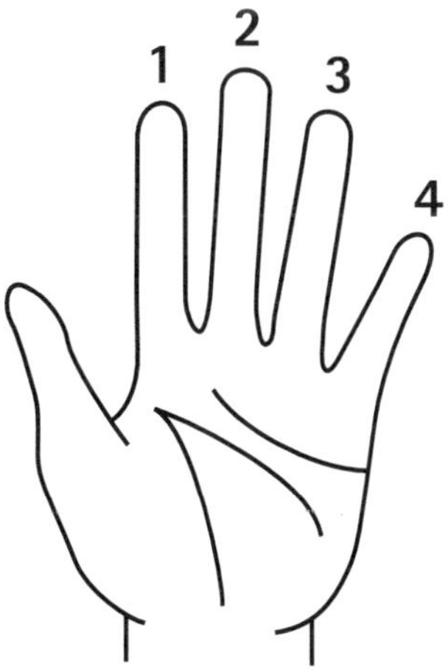

C CHORDS

C MAJOR
[C]

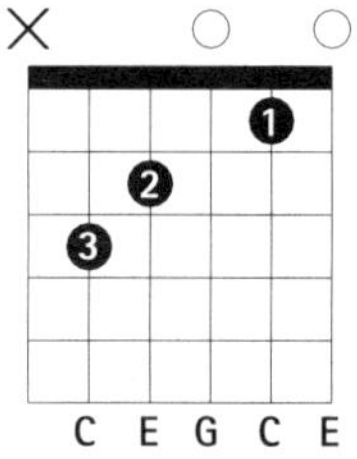

C MINOR
[Cm, Cmi, C–]

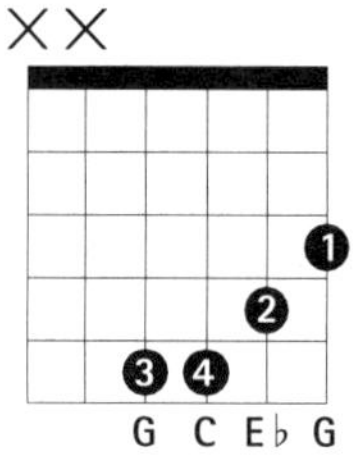

C SIXTH
[C6]

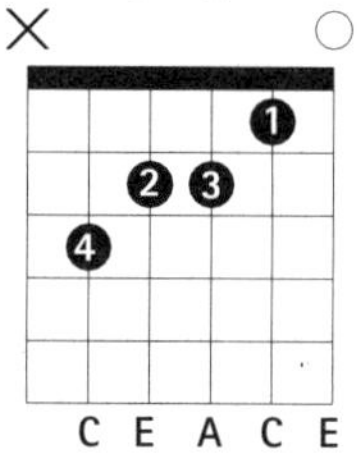

C SEVENTH
[C7]

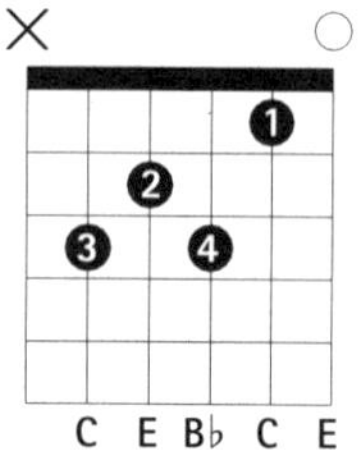

C MINOR SEVENTH
[Cm7, Cmi7, C–7]

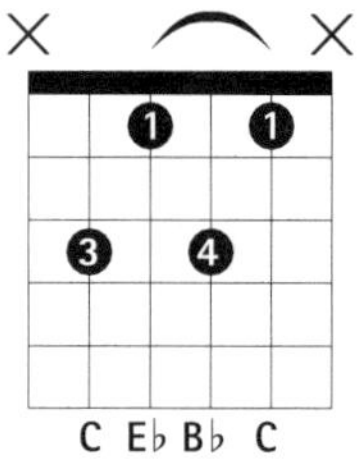

C NINTH
[C9]

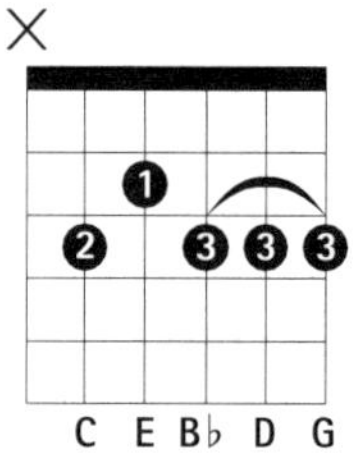

C AUGMENTED
[C+, Caug, C(♯5)]

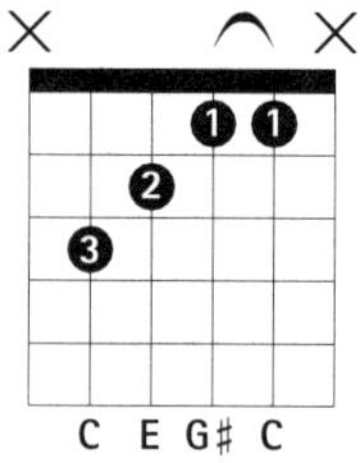

C DIMINISHED SEVENTH
[Cdim7, C°7, Cdim]

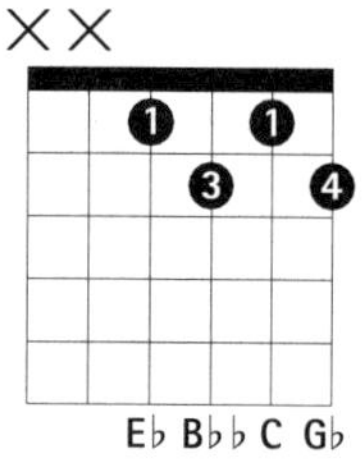

C♯/D♭ CHORDS

C♯ MAJOR
[C♯]

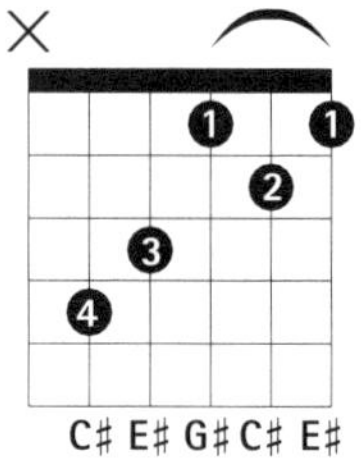

C♯ MINOR
[C♯m, C♯mi, C♯–]

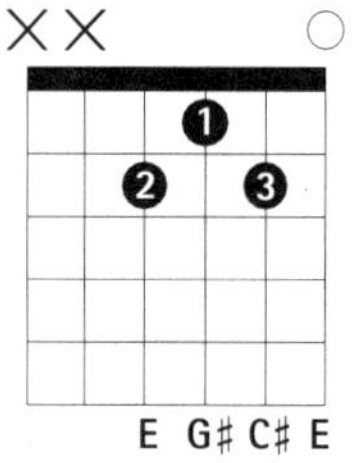

C♯ SIXTH
[C♯6]

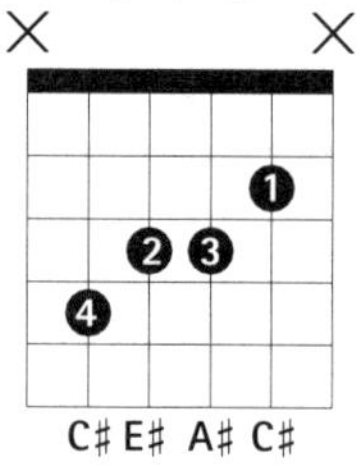

C♯ SEVENTH
[C♯7]

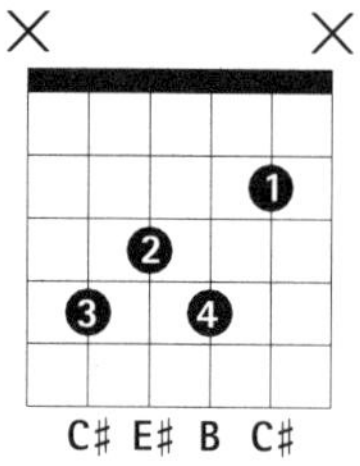

C♯ MINOR SEVENTH
[C♯m7, C♯mi7, C♯–7]

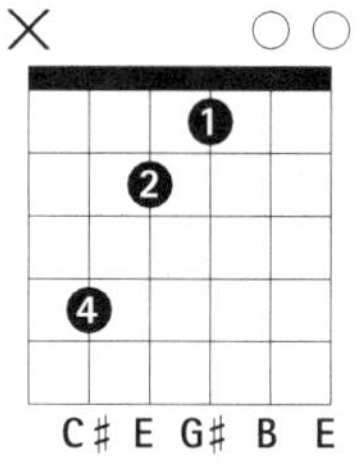

C♯ NINTH
[C♯9]

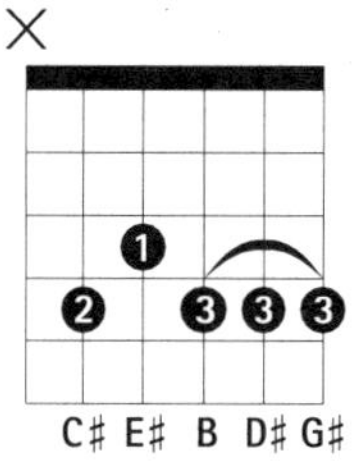

C♯ AUGMENTED
[C♯+, C♯aug, C♯(♯5)]

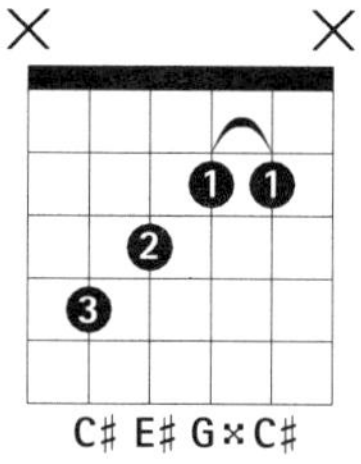

C♯ DIMINISHED SEVENTH
[C♯dim7, C♯°7, C♯dim]

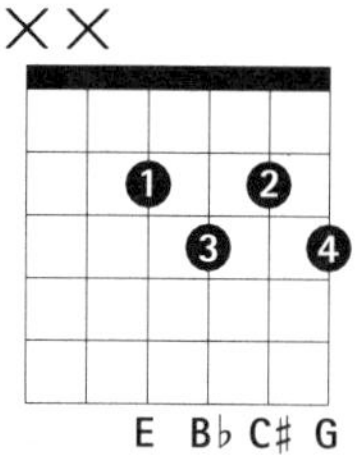

D CHORDS

D MAJOR
[D]

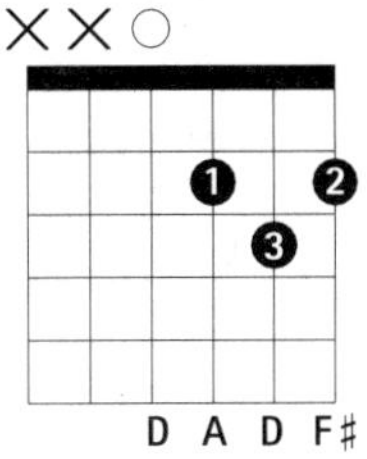

D MINOR
[Dm, Dmi, D-]

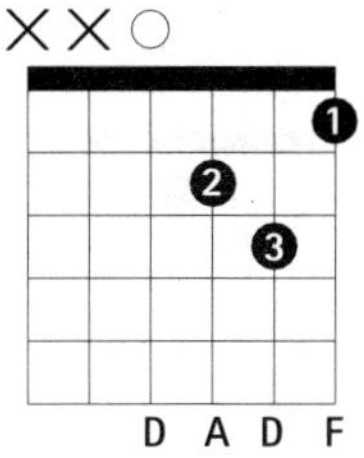

D SIXTH
[D6]

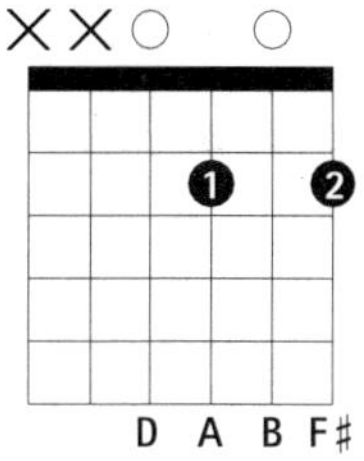

D SEVENTH
[D7]

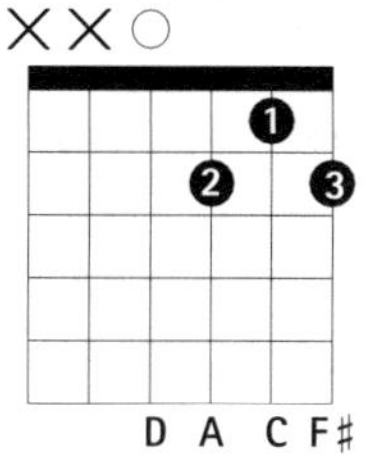

D MINOR SEVENTH
[Dm7, Dmi7, D-7]

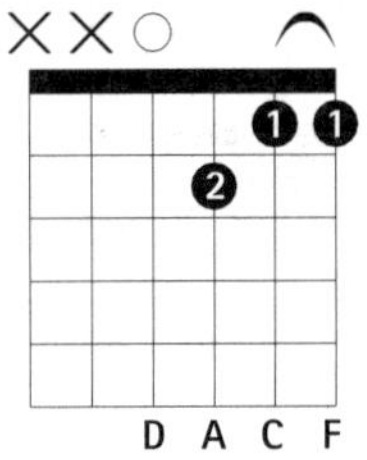

D NINTH
[D9]

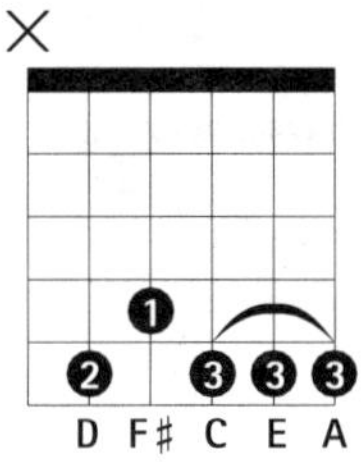

D AUGMENTED
[D+, Daug, D(♯5)]

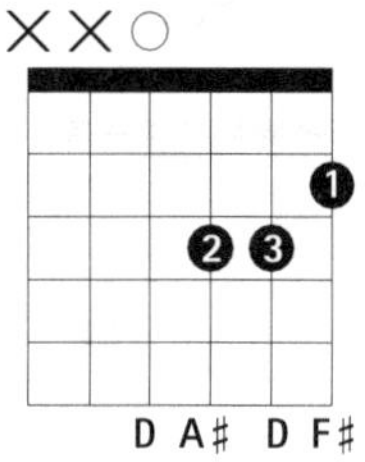

D DIMINISHED SEVENTH
[Ddim7, D°7, Ddim]

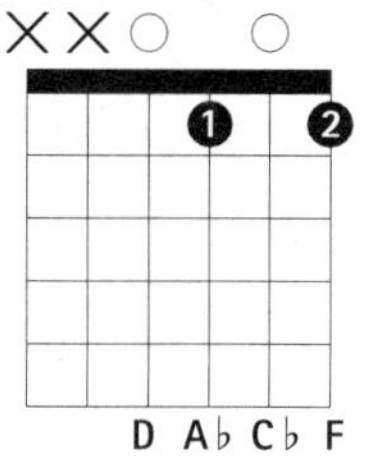

D♯/E♭ CHORDS

E♭ MAJOR
[E♭]

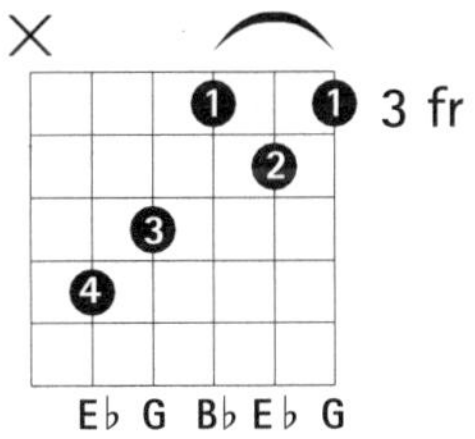

E♭ MINOR
[E♭m, E♭mi, E♭-]

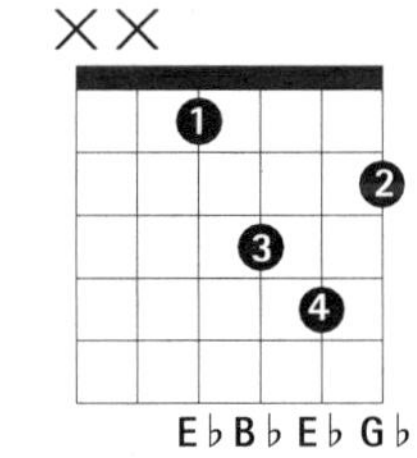

E♭ SIXTH
[E♭6]

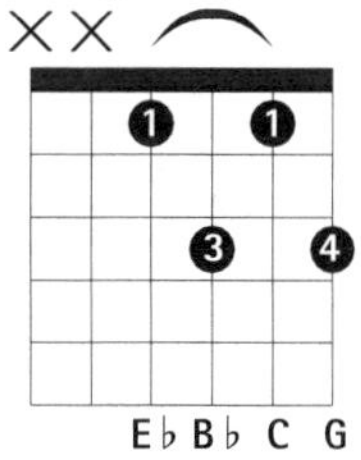

E♭ SEVENTH
[E♭7]

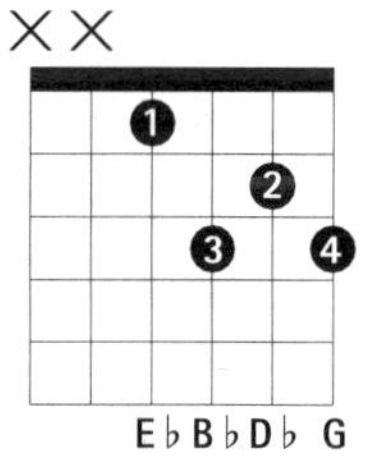

E♭ MINOR SEVENTH
[E♭m7, E♭mi7, E♭-7]

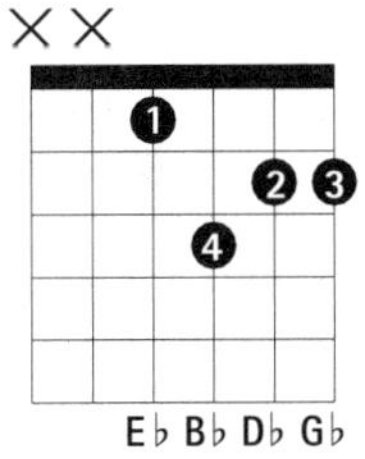

E♭ NINTH
[E♭9]

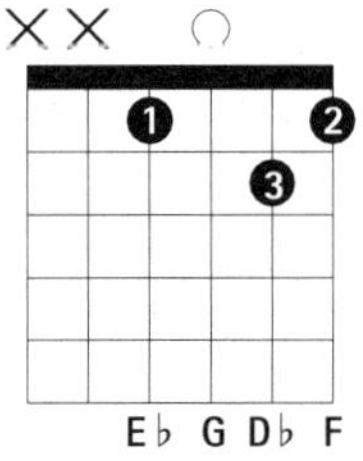

E♭ AUGMENTED
[E♭+, E♭aug, E♭(♯5)]

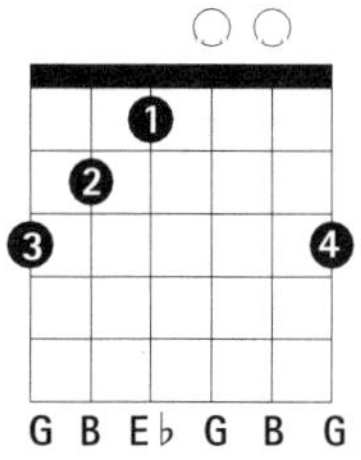

E♭ DIMINISHED SEVENTH
[E♭dim7, E♭°7, E♭dim]

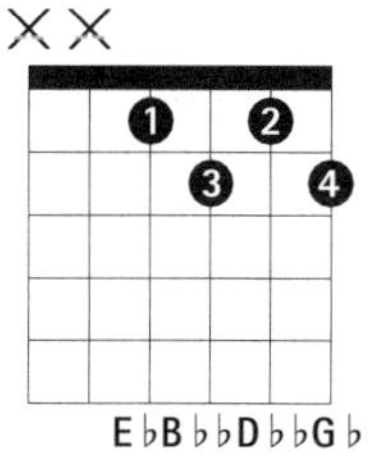

E CHORDS

E MAJOR
[E]

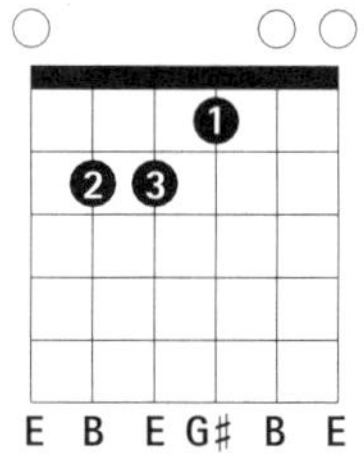

E MINOR
[Em, Emi, E–]

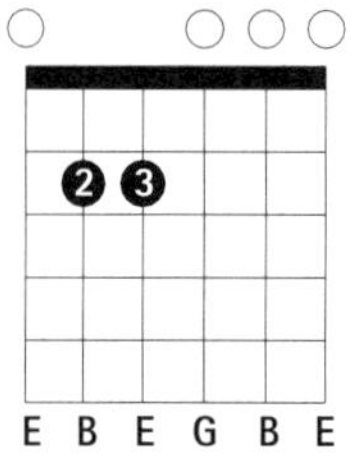

E SIXTH
[E6]

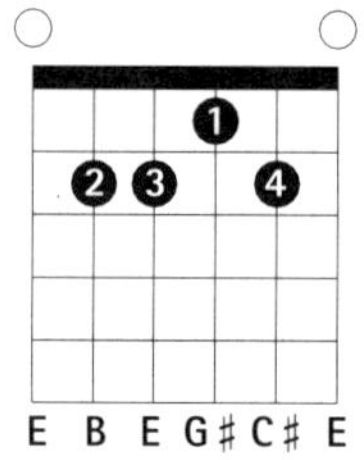

E SEVENTH
[E7]

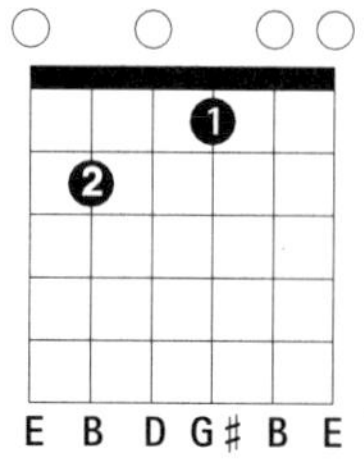

E MINOR SEVENTH
[Em7, Emi7, E–7]

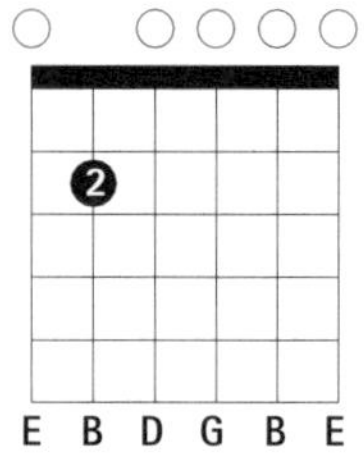

E NINTH
[E9]

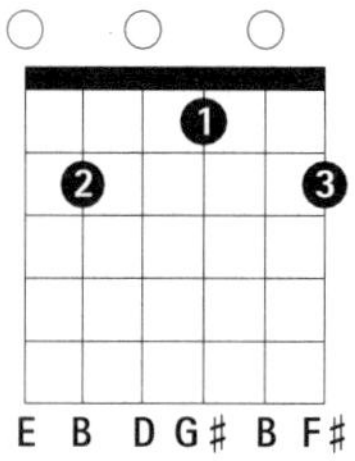

E AUGMENTED
[E+, Eaug, E(♯5)]

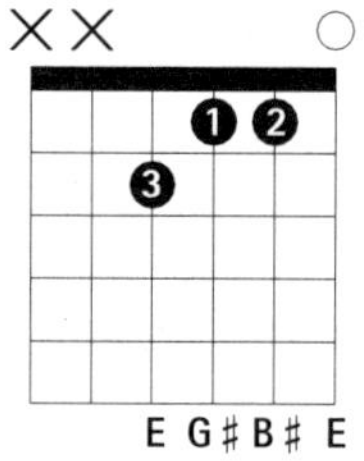

E DIMINISHED SEVENTH
[Edim7, E°7, Edim]

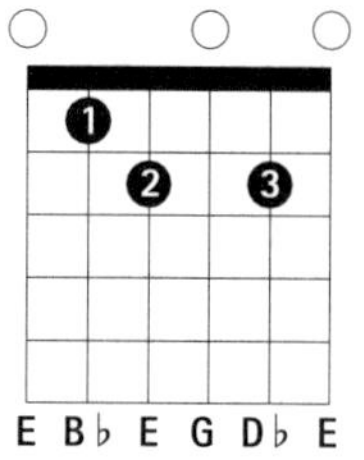

F CHORDS

F MAJOR
[F]

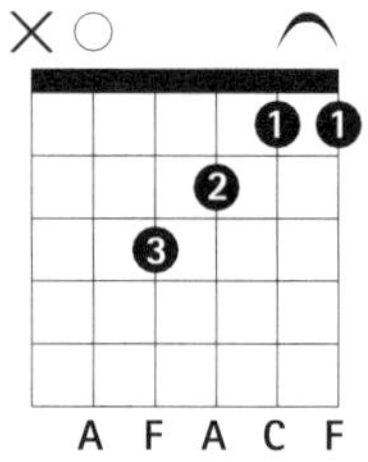

F MINOR
[Fm, Fmi, F–]

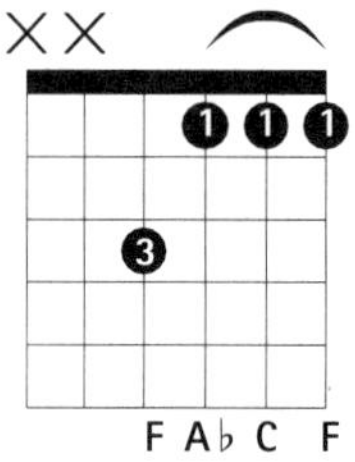

F SIXTH
[F6]

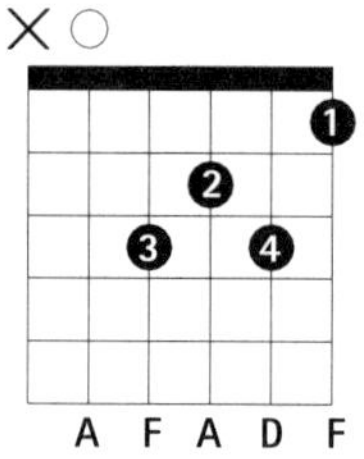

F SEVENTH
[F7]

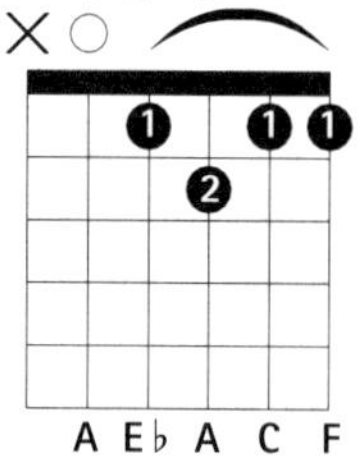

F MINOR SEVENTH
[Fm7, Fmi7, F–7]

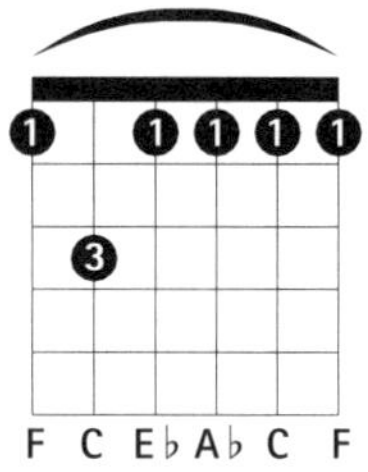

F NINTH
[F9]

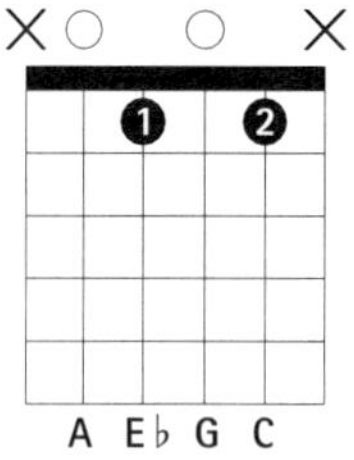

F AUGMENTED
[F+, Faug, F(♯5)]

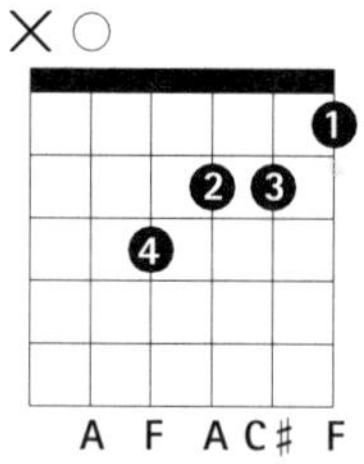

F DIMINISHED SEVENTH
[Fdim7, F°7, Fdim]

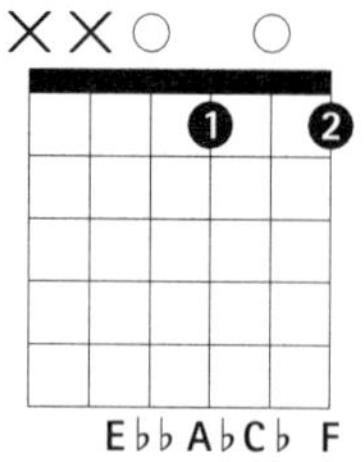

F♯/G♭ CHORDS

F♯ MAJOR
[F♯]

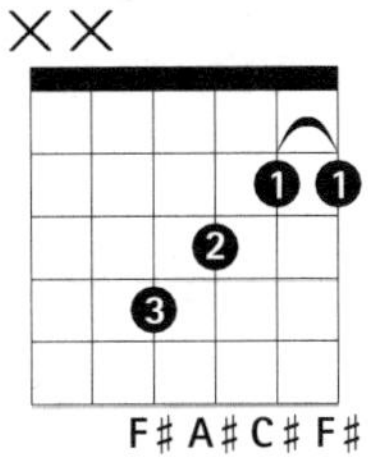

F♯ MINOR
[F♯m, F♯mi, F♯–]

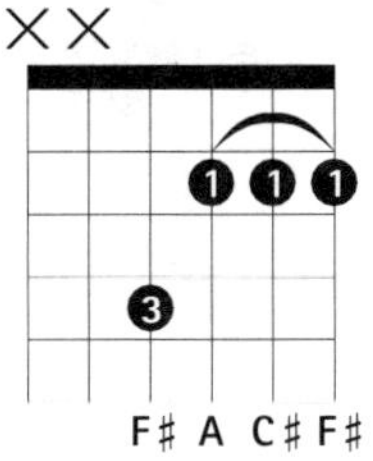

F♯ SIXTH
[F♯6]

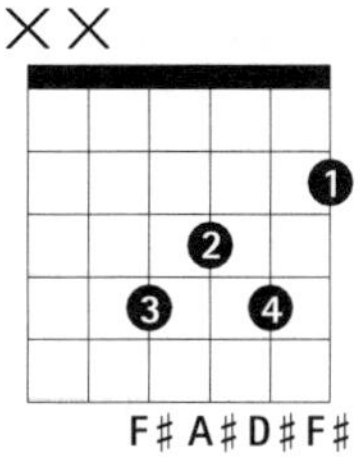

F♯SEVENTH
[F♯7]

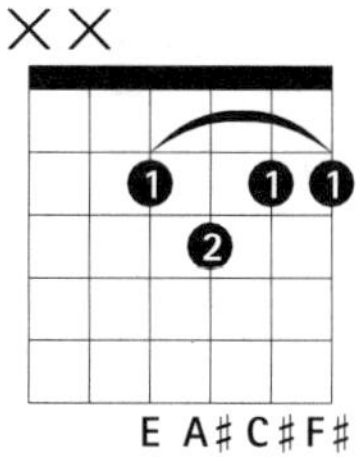

F♯ MINOR SEVENTH
[F♯m7, F♯mi7, F♯–7]

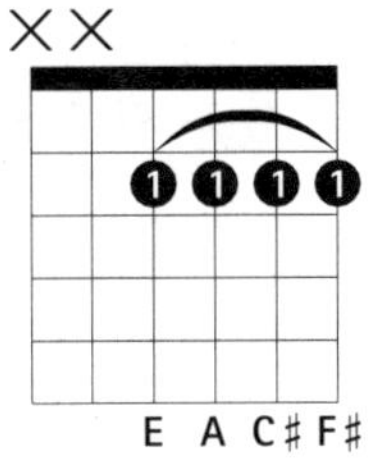

F♯ NINTH
[F♯9]

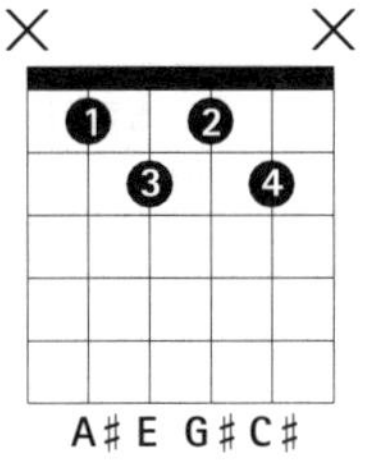

F♯ AUGMENTED
[F♯+, F♯aug, F♯(♯5)]

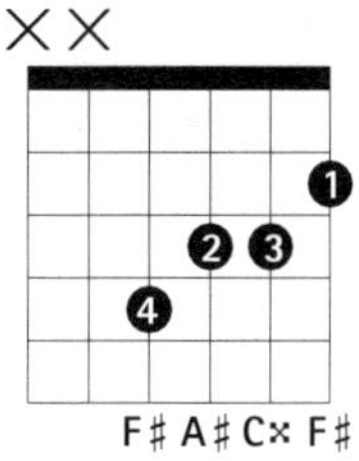

F♯ DIMINISHED SEVENTH
[F♯dim7, F♯°7, F♯dim]

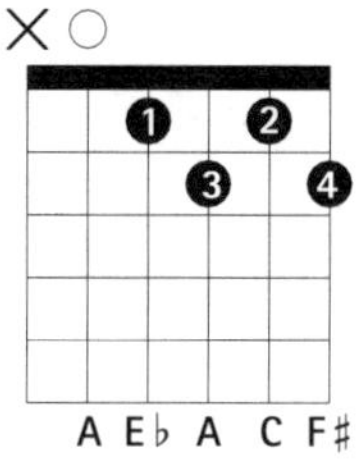

G CHORDS

G MAJOR
[G]

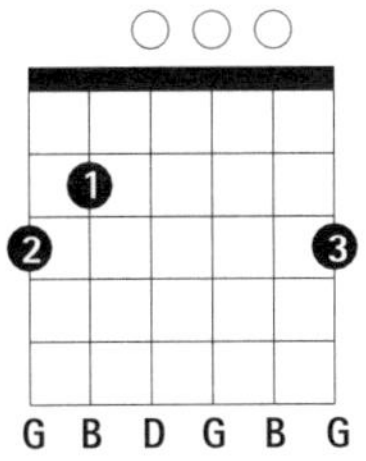

G MINOR
[Gm, Gmi, G–]

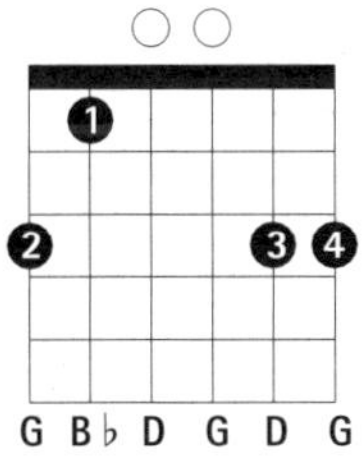

G SIXTH
[G6]

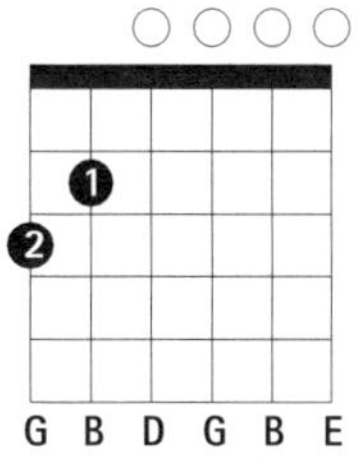

G SEVENTH
[G7]

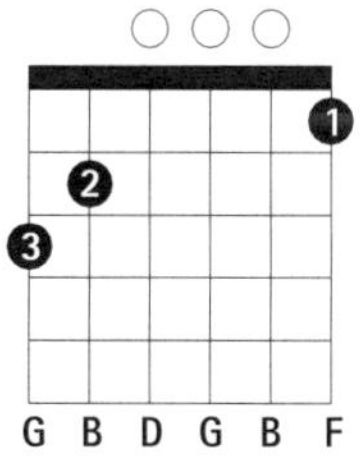

G MINOR SEVENTH
[Gm7, Gmi7, G–7]

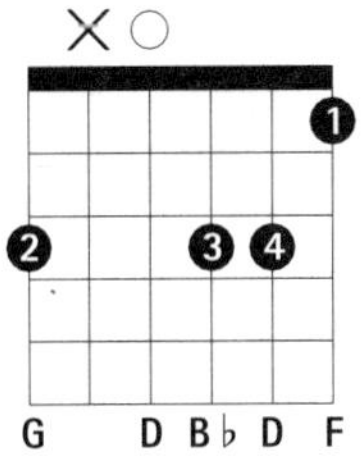

G NINTH
[G9]

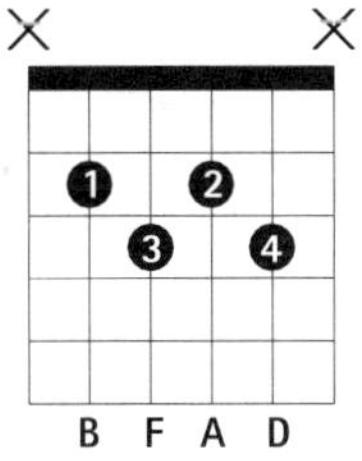

G AUGMENTED
[G+, Gaug, G(♯5)]

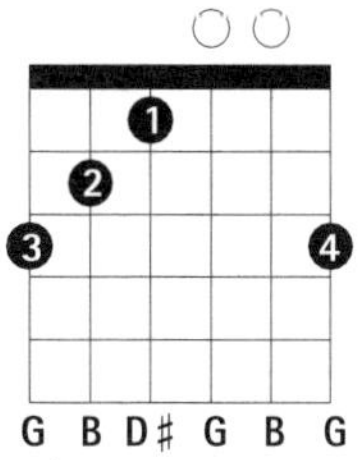

G DIMINISHED SEVENTH
[Gdim7, G°7, Gdim]

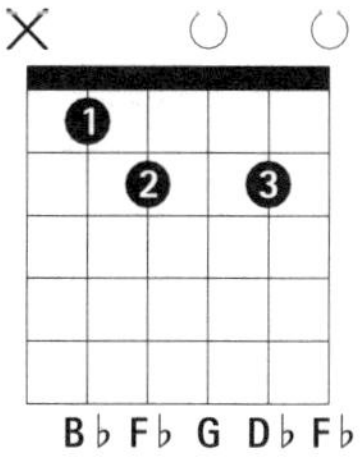

G♯/A♭ CHORDS

A♭ MAJOR
[A♭]

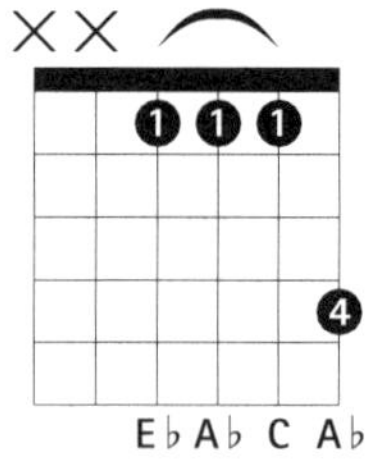

A♭ MINOR
[A♭m, A♭mi, A♭-]

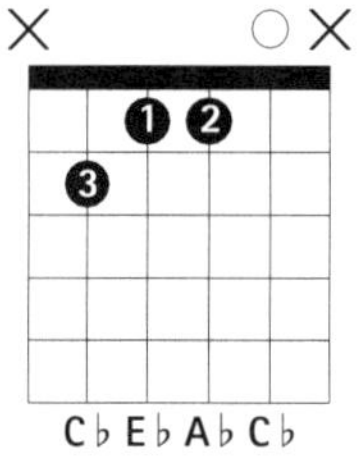

A♭ SIXTH
[A♭6]

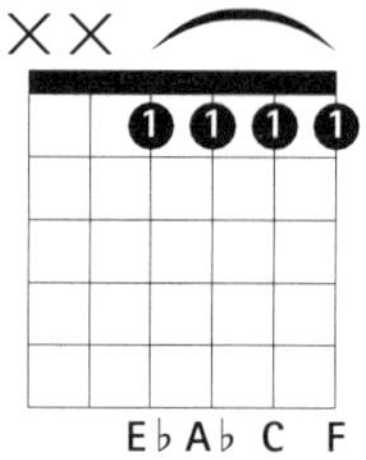

A♭ SEVENTH
[A♭7]

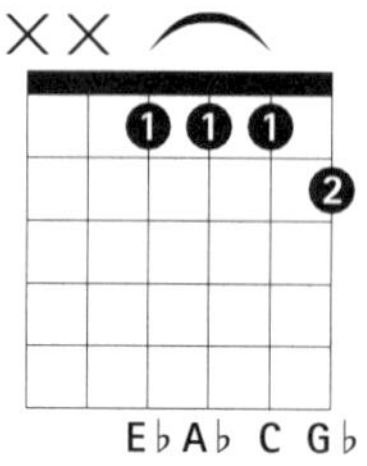

A♭ MINOR SEVENTH
[A♭m7, A♭mi7, A♭-7]

A♭ NINTH
[A♭9]

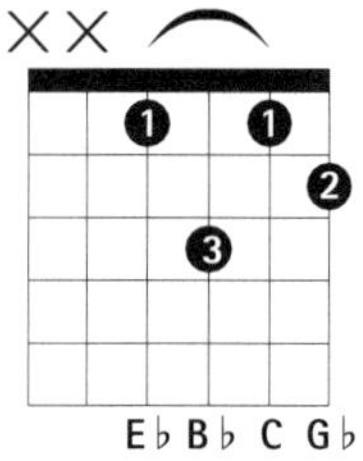

A♭ AUGMENTED
[A♭+, A♭aug, A♭(♯5)]

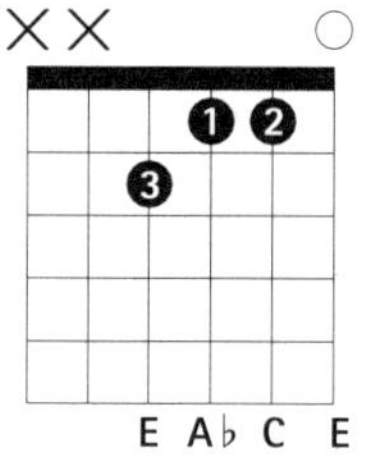

A♭ DIMINISHED SEVENTH
[A♭dim7, A♭°7, A♭dim]

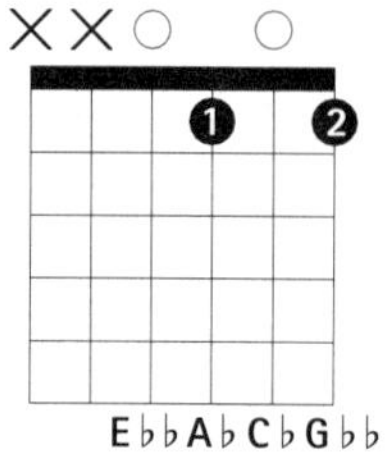

A CHORDS

A MAJOR
[A]

A MINOR
[Am, Ami, A-]

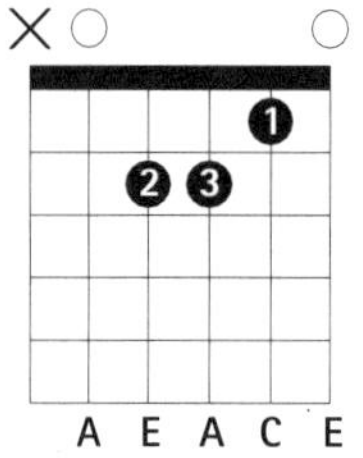

A SIXTH
[A6]

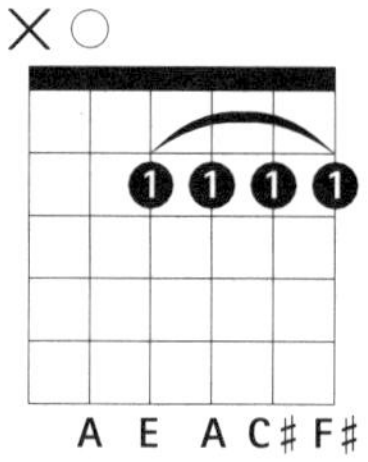

A SEVENTH
[A7]

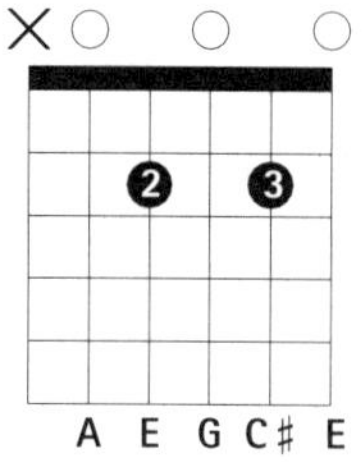

A MINOR SEVENTH
[Am7, Ami7, A-7]

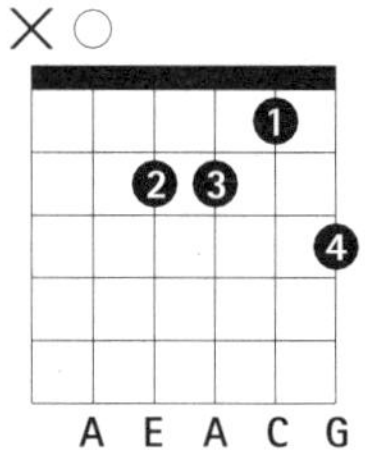

A NINTH
[A9]

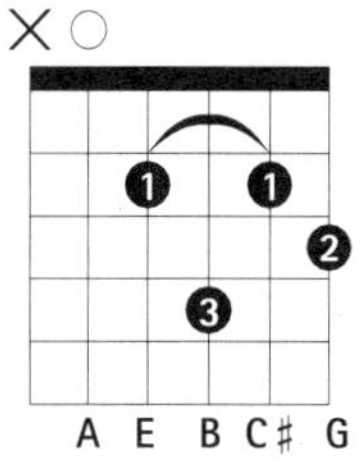

A AUGMENTED
[A+, Aaug, A(♯5)]

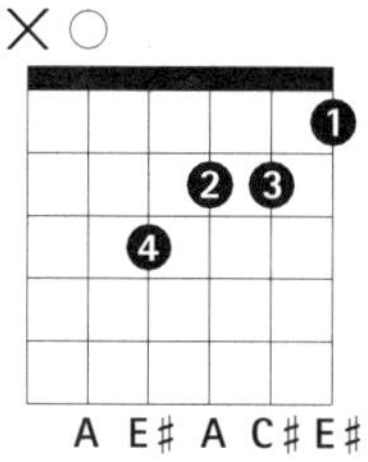

A DIMINISHED SEVENTH
[Adim7, A°7, Adim]

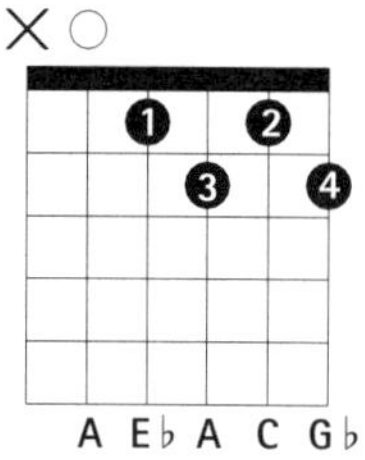

A♯/B♭ CHORDS

B♭ MAJOR
[B♭]

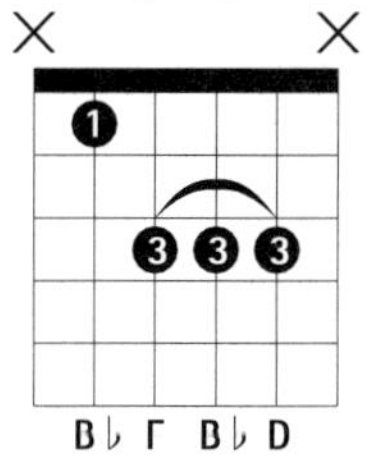

B♭ MINOR
[B♭m, B♭mi, B♭-]

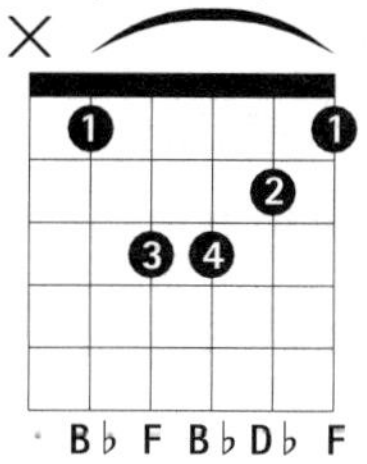

B♭ SIXTH
[B♭6]

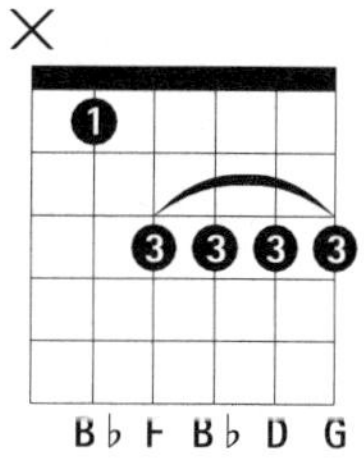

B♭ SEVENTH
[B♭7]

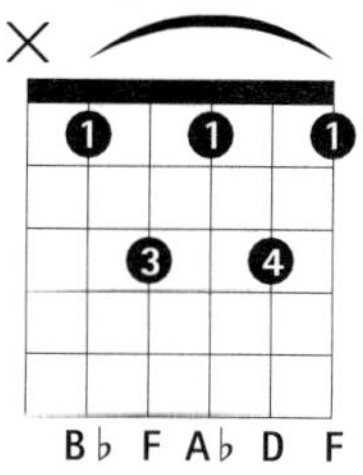

B♭ MINOR SEVENTH
[B♭m7, B♭mi7, B♭-7]

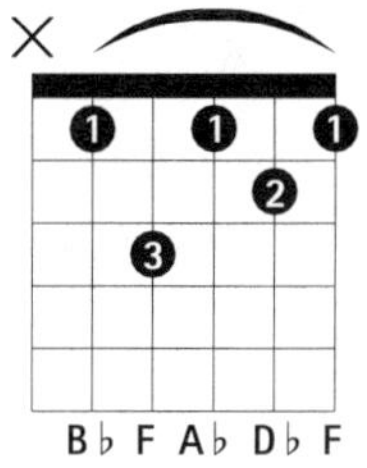

B♭ NINTH
[B♭9]

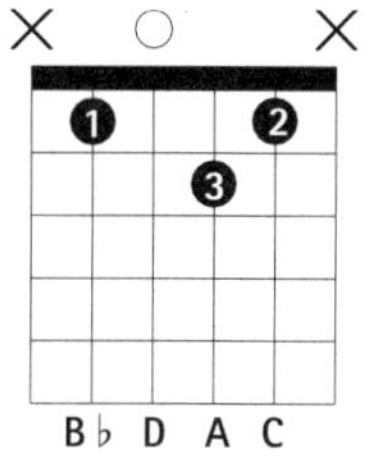

B♭ AUGMENTED
[B♭+, B♭aug, B♭(♯5)]

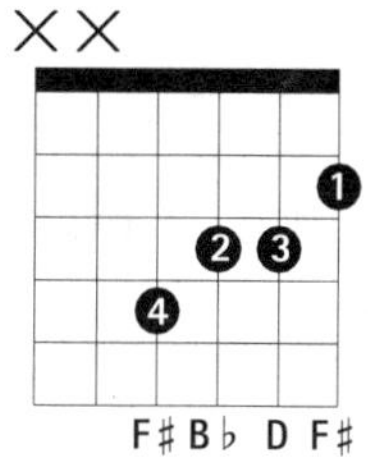

B♭ DIMINISHED SEVENTH
[B♭dim7, B♭°7, B♭dim]

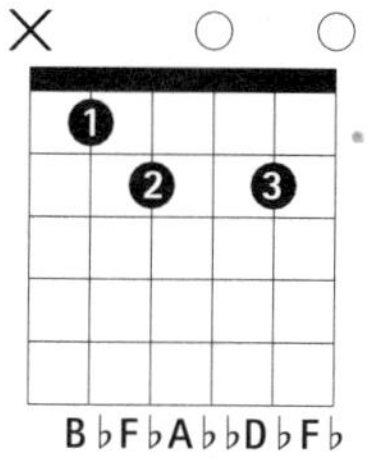

B CHORDS

B MAJOR
[B]

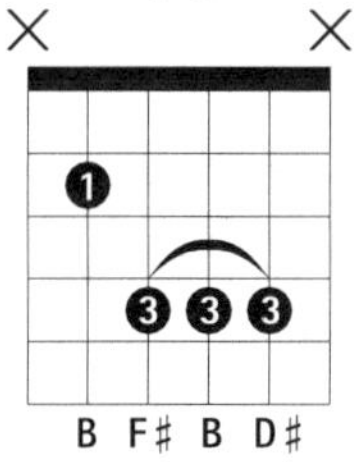

B MINOR
[Bm, Bmi, B-]

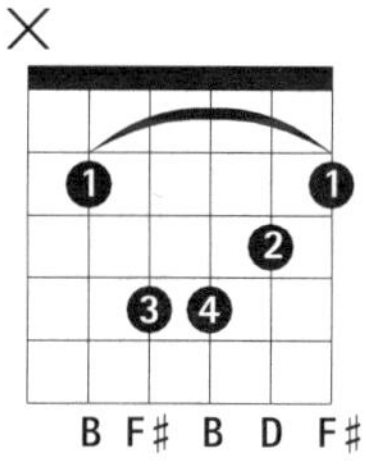

B SIXTH
[B6]

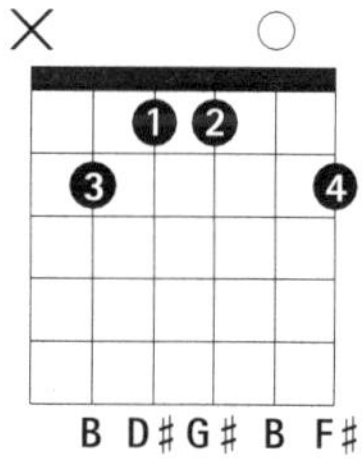

B SEVENTH
[B7]

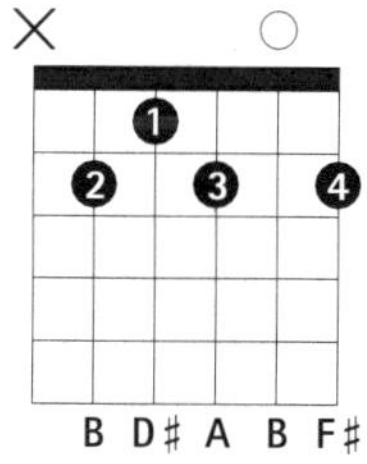

B MINOR SEVENTH
[Bm7, Bmi7, B-7]

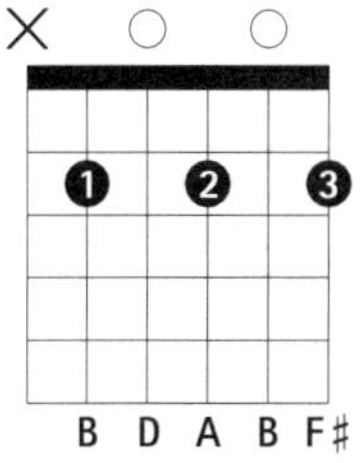

B NINTH
[B9]

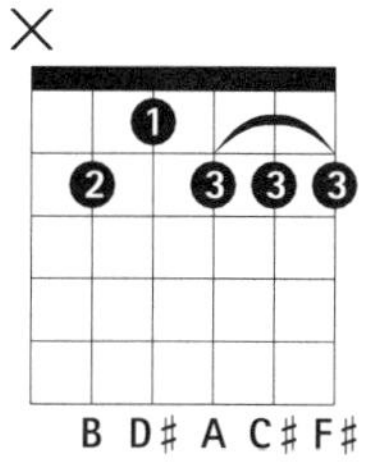

B AUGMENTED
[B+, Baug, B(♯5)]

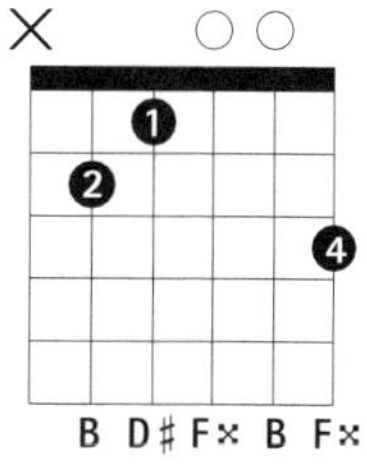

B DIMINISHED SEVENTH
[Bdim7, B°7, Bdim]

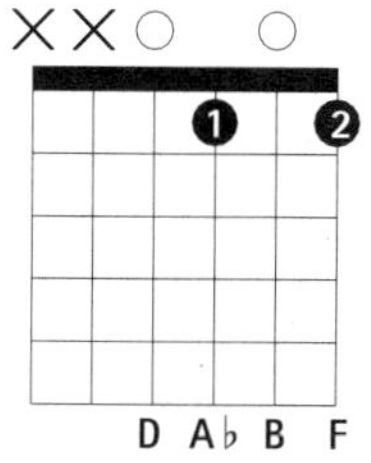

BARRE CHORDS

Barre chords are among the most useful things in all guitardom. The first finger holds down all six strings, while the remaining three fingers make a chord shape. Barre chords make it easy to play in any key. The first finger acts like a capo. If a song calls for a G♯ minor chord, for example, there's no need to rack your brains to try and remember the open shape for that chord. Just slap your first finger down on the fourth fret while the other fingers form an E minor shape. And, stylistically speaking, barre chords are integral to the sound of rock and roll—from Chuck Berry to the Ramones to the Smashing Pumpkins.

The most frequently used family of barre chords is based around open E chord shapes. The fingering, however, is a little different than what you'd use for an open E:

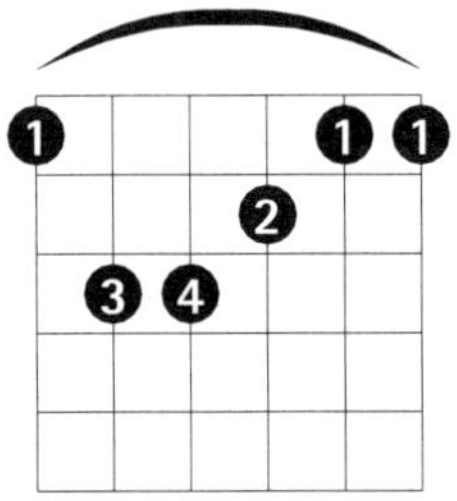
E shape

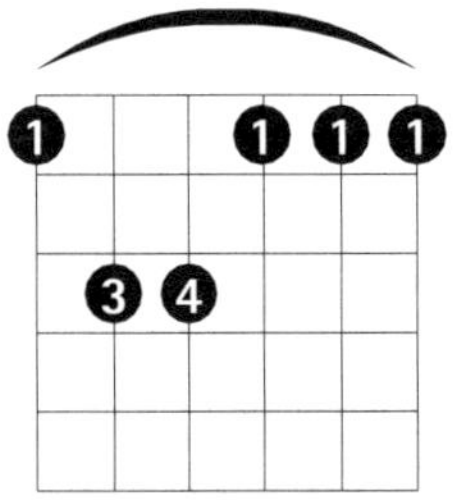
Em shape

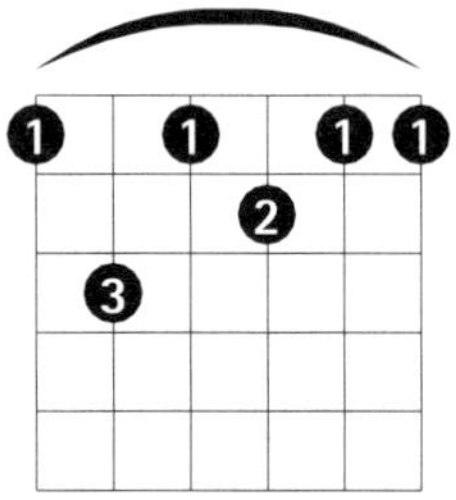
E7 shape

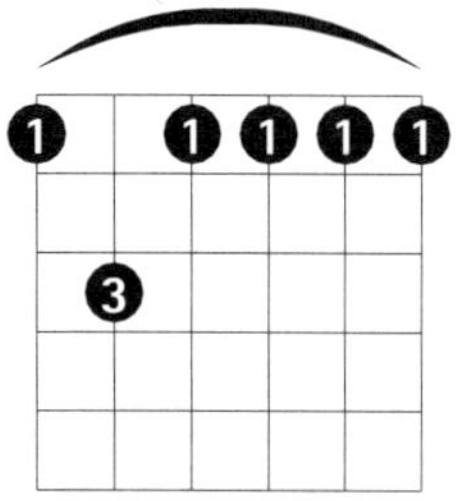
Em7 shape

Barre chords based around open A chord shapes are also very useful and frequently employed:

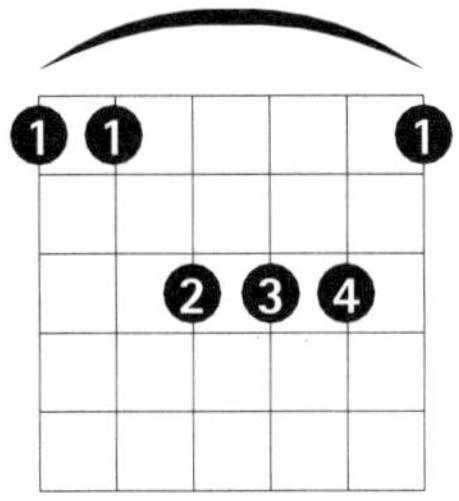
A shape

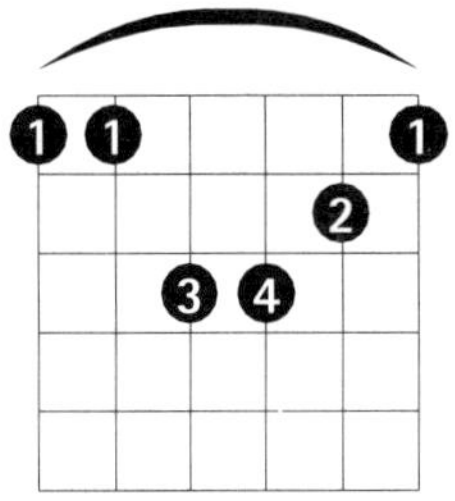
Am shape

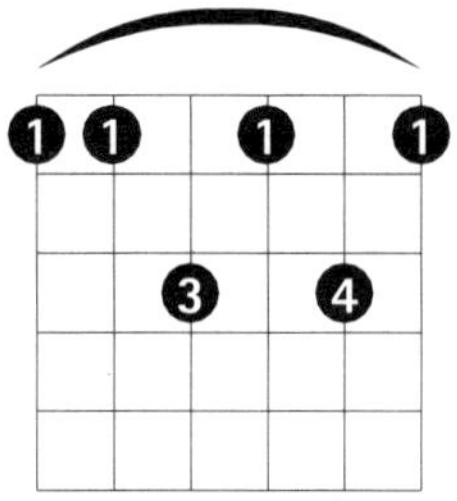
A7 shape

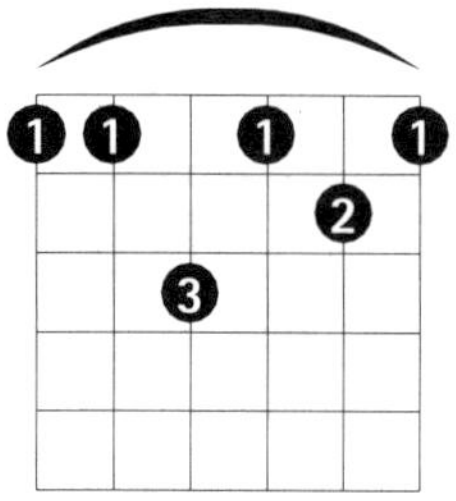
Am7 shape

Barre chords can also be built on the C and G open chord shapes:

Barre chords enable guitarists to do something called position playing. Without moving the first finger barre, it's possible to play entire chord progressions and to voice chords in the same region of the neck where a melody is being played.

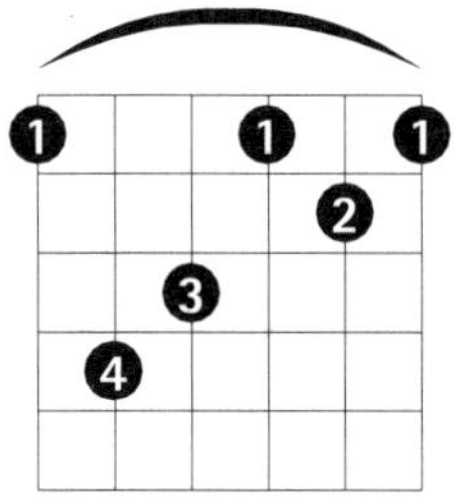
C shape

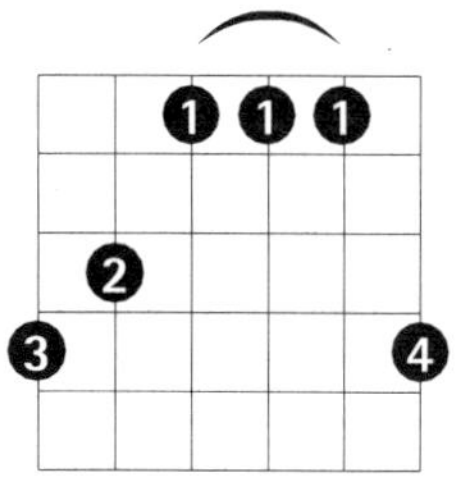
G shape

TABLATURE

Tablature dates back to the Renaissance and was used by lutanists, guitarists, and other stringed instrument players. It had fallen into obscurity by the time the twentieth century rolled around, but was revived, strange to say, by the shred metal boom of the 1980s. "Tab" proved an ideal medium for guitar magazines to use in showing aspiring Yngwies where to put their fingers in order to duplicate the blazing, scorching, awesome, and jaw-dropping riffage of their spandex heroes. Today it is in widespread use for many styles.

In essence, tablature does for riffs and melodies what chord charts do for chords. It provides a graphic display of string and fret information. What it doesn't convey is timing information: time signature, tempo, phrasing, and durations of notes. It is therefore best used as an aid in playing music that the guitarist is already familiar with from a record or some other source, and is most often used in conjunction with conventional notation.

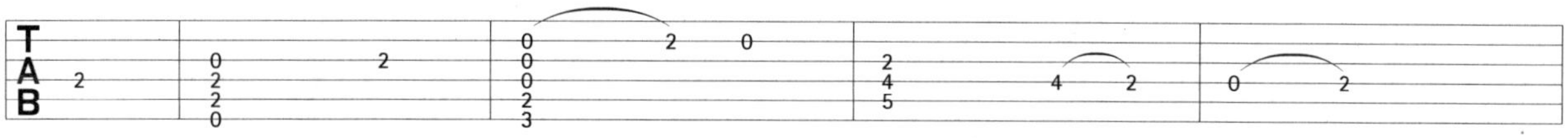

Horizontal lines represent the strings. The fattest (sixth string) is at the bottom; the thinnest (first string) is at the top.

Numerals indicate which fret to play on the string indicated.

A curved line connecting two numerals indicates a hammer-on (going from a low fret to a higher one) or a pull-off (going from a higher fret to a lower one).

Two or more numerals vertically aligned indicate notes that should be played simultaneously.

CONVENTIONAL NOTATION

A good knowledge of conventional notation will allow you to play pieces that you've never heard before, just by reading what's on the page. All the necessary information is there: the rhythmic value of the notes, as well as their pitches. Unlike tab, conventional notation provides visual cues that allow the player to anticipate what lies ahead. Is the melody ascending or descending? Is there a big burst of short, fast notes coming up? Or a passage where the performer will "lay out" and not play anything?

Conventional notation was not specially devised for the guitar; it contains no information about the strings. But it can provide fingering cues via the finger numbering system given above. If you have a good command of where the notes lie on the fretboard, this should be enough.

PITCH

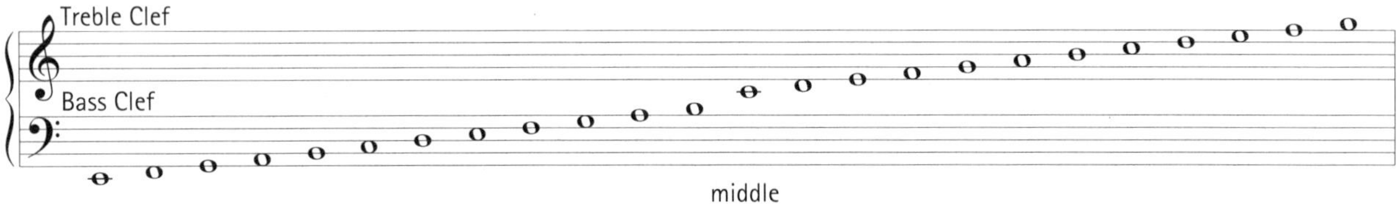

E F G **A** B C **D** E F **G** A **B** C D **E** F G A B C D E F G

(**Boldface** letters = open strings on guitar)

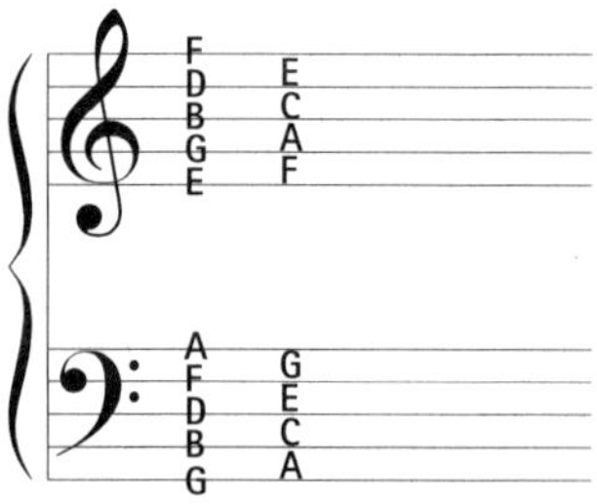

In conventional notation, the horizontal lines and spaces represent pitches, from low to high. The upper-register pitches are represented in the treble clef; the lower ones are represented in the bass clef. Most of the guitar's range falls in the bass clef. But to keep the notes within a single clef, most guitar music is written in the treble clef, an octave higher than it actually sounds.

A musical staff has five lines and four spaces. Each one represents a different pitch. In the treble clef, the lines from bottom to top represent these notes:
E–G–B–D–F
Beginning music students are taught a little phrase to help them remember these: **Every Good Boy Does Fine.** (Or, if you learned in England: **Every Good Boy Deserves Favour**. Of course, these sayings were coined in simpler times. Present-day feminists and other gender-sensitive types might prefer: **Every Girl Bassist Does Fine.**)

The notes represented by the treble clef spaces conveniently spell out a nice, politically neutral word:
F–A–C–E

In the bass clef, the notes on the lines are:
G–B–D–F–A
The schoolroom mnemonic device for this one is not terribly logical: **Great Big Dogs Fight Animals.** Of course, great big dogs *are* animals; but maybe it's best not to look too deeply into these things.

The notes associated with the bass clef spaces are:
A–C–E–G
You can master these if you can remember that **All Cows Eat Grass.**

Pitches that are higher or lower than the notes on a staff are indicated by means of **ledger lines**:

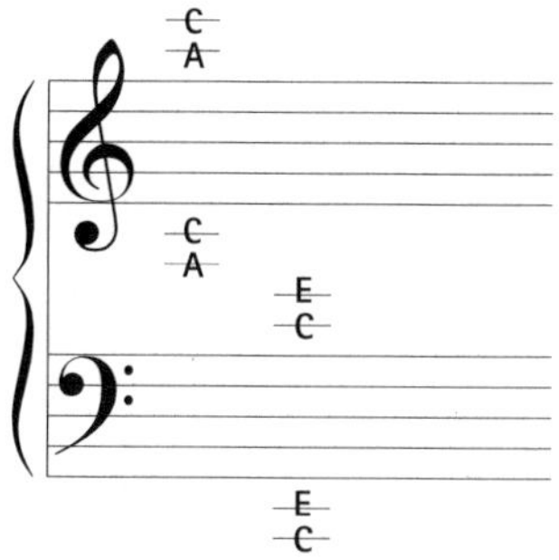

When a note is preceded by a **sharp** sign (♯), its pitch should be raised one half step (one fret). When a note is preceded by a **flat** sign (♭), its pitch should be lowered one half step (one fret).

A note that is neither sharp nor flat is referred to as **natural**. A sharp or a flat can be canceled with a natural sign (♮).

A song with no sharps or flats (i.e., all naturals) is in the key of C major or A minor (which is what's called the **relative minor** of C major). In other keys, the same note or notes will ordinarily always be sharp or flat every time they occur, depending on what the key is. All this is spelled out at the beginning of the song, right next to the clef, in something called the **key signature**:

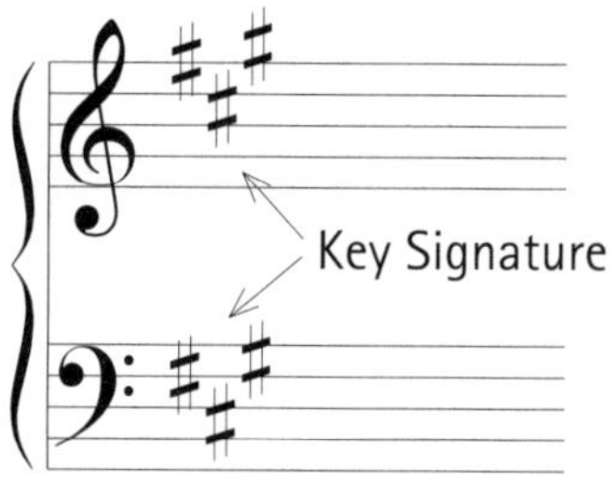

By counting the sharps or flats in the key signature, you can know what key a song is in.

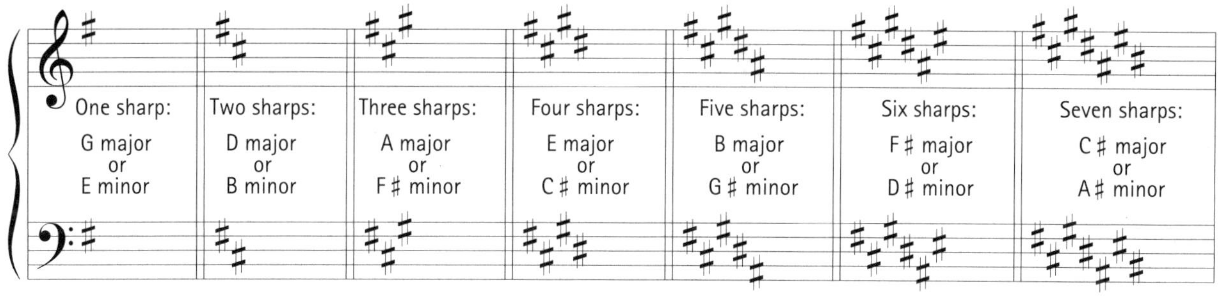

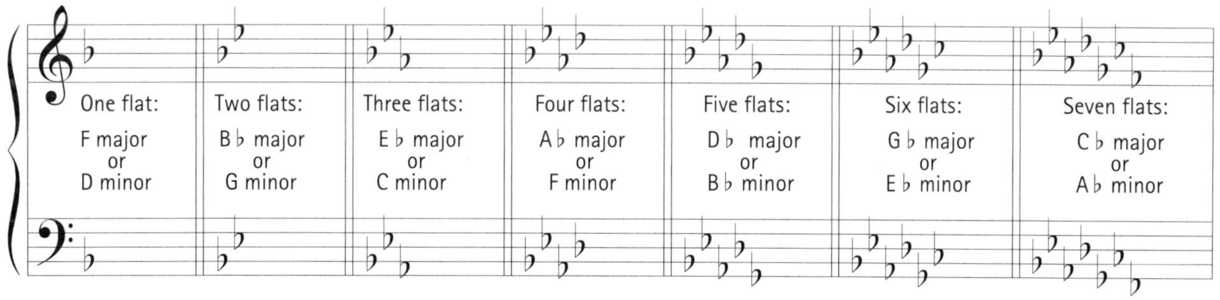

A sharp, flat, or natural sign next to a note (as opposed to in the key signature) is called an **accidental**.

RHYTHM

The appearance of each note indicates how long it should be sounded:

Rests indicate silences—places where the instrument doesn't sound. Their time values correspond to the different note values:

So just how long does whole note last? Or a half, or a quarter,...? These questions are answered by the **time signature**, which is given at the beginning of the song, right next to the key signature:

The top number indicates how many **beats** will be in each **measure** (also called a **bar**).

The bottom number indicates which **note value** equals one beat. In this case, it's the quarter note.

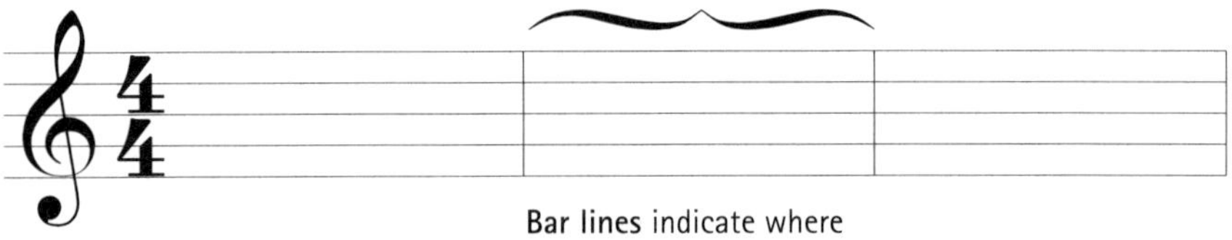

The most commonly used time signature, particularly in pop music, is 4/4. Which is why it is sometimes called **common time**. Another familiar time signature is 3/4, or **waltz time**. Other time signatures are generally the domain of prog rock, fusion, or other styles where the musicians get insulted if people want to dance.

The word **tempo** is Italian for "time." In music, it refers to the pace at which a piece is played—fast, slow, or in between. Tempo can be measured in **beats per minute (bpm)**. Some printed music includes an indication of tempo (printed at the top of the first staff, over the time and key signatures), stating the value of a quarter note in beats per minute:

♩ = 120

If you're practicing with a metronome or drum machine, simply dial it to the appropriate bpm setting to find out exactly how fast or slow a piece was meant to be played.

EDDIE VAN HALEN

© Eddie Mallok / Retna LTD.

On other printed music, however, you'll find only a verbal indication of tempo. These directions are often given in Italian, since Italy was a hugely influential music place (kind of like Seattle in the early nineties) back when they made all this stuff up hundreds of years ago:

Presto—very fast

Allegro—fast, lively

Moderato—moderate

Andante—moderate to slow

Adagio—slow

Lento—very slow

As Italian is a marvelously expressive language, you'll find many variations of these basic terms, indicating subtle shadings of tempo: a lively allegro (**Allegro vivace**); a tranquil allegro (**Allegro tranquillo**); allegro, but not too much (**Allegro non troppo**); allegro with oomph (**Allegro con brio**); allegro with linguine (only joking); ...there are dozens of 'em. Like all language, these words are subject to interpretation and grow familiar with experience.

Sometimes you'll also find printed directions to speed up or slow down the tempo in the middle of a piece. A gradual increase in tempo is called an **accellerando** and is usually abbreviated as **Accel.** in printed music. **Rit. (ritardando)** and **Rall. (rallentando)** are both commands to slow down. **A tempo** means to return to the original tempo.

STONE GOSSARD

© T. Stone / Retna LTD.

the creative guitarist

INSPIRATION

They say that creativity is 1 percent inspiration and 99 percent perspiration. Brilliant musical ideas tend to come in a flash, but it generally takes a lot of hard work to transform those flashes into actual notes on the page, stage, or disc. The 99 percent hard work factor tends to remain constant whether you're constructing a solo, writing a song, or trying to come up with an inventive accompaniment part. Inspiration is the mysterious part of the equation. Where does it come from? Can it be summoned at will? Different guitarists have different ways of explaining it.

"Half the battle is with your ego: to find something you think is cool to play. And then the other half is just having something inspire you in a way you haven't heard before." ...Stone Gossard

MOVING BEYOND TECHNIQUE

Every guitarist starts out grappling with the basic, physical problems of technique. How to stretch the fingers to play a B7 chord. How to bend a note. Technique is the first hurdle. Some beginners find the requisite motor skills too daunting and conclude the guitar is just not for them. But if you make it past this first barrier, the day inevitably arrives when you've acquired enough technique to make your own creative statement with the guitar. How much technique is enough? That depends on the statement you want to make. The great folksinger Woody Guthrie knew a handful of first-position chords and rarely, if ever, ventured higher than the third fret. Yet his songs will be sung and remembered long after many more accomplished guitarists have been forgotten. There is no direct correlation between technique and creativity. Nor can technique ever be a substitute for creativity.

Over-obsession with technique is one of the biggest sand traps in the great golf course of guitar playing. It's like one of those Freudian hangups where the patient fixates on some childhood phase in order to avoid the thornier issues of adulthood. Many guitarists find the prospect of coming up with an original idea far more frightening than having to play thirty-second-note arpeggios. But every guitarist should at least try to make that creative leap. Once you've mastered what you deem a sufficient amount of technique, your next task is to forget it. Don't lose it; just internalize it so that it becomes second nature to you—a subconscious impulse. When you pick up your guitar to play, technique shouldn't be foremost on your mind.

"I don't think of the mechanics of playing anymore. That's secondary to me. Einstein said that imagination is more important than knowledge. So practice your imagination."
...Carlos Santana

FAREWELL TO HEROES

As guitarists, we all start out imitating our heroes. It's a natural impulse. But this is another one of those things that a healthy, well-rounded guitarist should eventually outgrow. Once you've absorbed what you need from your heroes, it's time to go on and make your own creative statement. Of course, in most parts of America, copy bands can make more money than acts that play original music. You can derive a solid middle-class income from playing covers (and that's nothing to sneeze at), but you'll never enter the big sweepstakes. For a chance at stardom, or even cult hero status, you'll have to cook up something of your own.

Some musicians are lucky. Their imitation is so unlike the thing they're trying to imitate that they accidentally end up inventing a new style or sound. (Which is essentially what happened back in the sixties, when young white Englishmen tried to sound like wizened old Delta bluesmen.) Other players take in such a diverse spectrum of musical influences that they end up creating their own unique fusion. Still other guitarists go through a more painful process of "killing their heroes"—a deliberate rejection of the players they once loved. Of course, they can never completely purge themselves of their influences, and may one day come to re-embrace them. But they need to make that violent break in order to find their own style. And then again there are those guitarists who simply wake up one morning and discover that their heroes have led them to a peak from which they can see their own path lying clearly before them. It's okay to wear your influences on your sleeve. Just make sure the shirt is your own.

"The idea that 'I wrote that' or 'I created that' is an overblown, artistic sort of thing that people love to put on writing songs. It can screw you up. If you think that it's all down to you, you got another thing coming. You're just an antenna. You just better switch on at the right time." ...Keith Richards

"When I was really young, there were days when I would sit around and try to imitate all the techniques I could find. Later on, I stopped relying so much on technique. But because I did that so intensely when I was young, it's still there, should I ever need to call on it. So if I need to—which I know will never happen—I can conceivably do a Malmsteen riff on something." ...Dave Navarro

LETTING GO

But *how* do you do it? How do you make that creative leap and play something both stunning and original? Most musicians agree that it doesn't come from the conscious mind. You can't do it by willing it to happen or deliberately trying. It usually involves getting past the rational part of your psyche. This is a difficult thing for some people, because it involves relinquishing control, simply "letting it happen." Songwriters often talk about great melodies just popping into their heads out of nowhere, frequently when they've just woken up. Improvisational players talk about getting so caught up in the flow of the music that they're no longer aware of their fingers moving on their instrument. A lot of musicians say the great ideas are out there "in the air" someplace; if you're receptive, you can pick up on them—like a radio.

"When I go into the studio, I don't necessarily know exactly what I'm going to try and accomplish that day. It usually ends up taking on a life of its own. I will basically fill up as many tracks as are available with guitar ideas. Then I like to step back and edit what I've done—tossing some ideas out, adding others. I prefer that to going into the studio with a concrete idea and trying to accomplish that. Because I found that, if I have a concrete idea of what I want, I usually can't get it anyway. So I throw my hands in the air and let the part take on a life of its own. On certain days, I might try something that I would never dream of trying the next day. It's nice to try and get all those ideas down and then see which ones work best." ...Dave Navarro

"So many guitarists today have had a flying start listening to Hendrix and Van Halen and all those guys, and it keeps breeding new generations of guitar players. It's a good thing, too. If [guitar playing] had died out ten years ago, I'd be working on cars for a living." ...Jeff Beck

"A lot of times, if you ask a guitarist about something great they played, they'll say, 'I don't even know how I played that.' It just seemed to flow through them. Like they were a conduit." ...Buddy Guy

CREATIVE BLOCKS

Most, if not all, musicians and songwriters go through "dry spells"—periods of time when the ideas just don't seem to be flowing. Because inspiration is such a mercurial thing, not subject to conscious control, this can be a frustrating, frightening experience. Some artists start to fear that they've "lost it" for good. Creative blocks can sometimes be traced to something else that's happening in your life: a personal crisis or problem, depression, even physical illness. In some cases, just realizing this is a big step toward removing the block. But at other times, there doesn't seem to be any cause. For reasons known only to themselves, the Muses sometimes just decide to take a powder. Don't panic. They'll be back. Barring extreme physical trauma or complete mental breakdown, good guitarists and songwriters don't just "lose it" for the rest of their lives. But most do experience blocks at some time or another. Some even develop their own personal strategies for getting past them.

"Sometimes I get writer's block. But you know how I cure that? I go to an art gallery. The first real training I had creatively was as [a visual] artist. And whenever anything creative comes along that baffles me, I go to a gallery, and it helps me adjust and see the world in some perspective. I think the secret of writer's blocks is that it happens when you lose your feeling for structure. It has to do with a loss of order, loss of parameters, or loss of perspective. So go back and read a book that's well constructed, or even listen to a great record that's perfectly put together, and it can do the same thing." ...Ray Davies

"There have been few times when I've had a breakthrough in my approach to music, theoretically. And it has always taken many painstaking hours to get through this barrier—to connect my old ideas with new ideas. Sometimes it's hard to advance without destroying what you already know. Many of us go through this. I've gone through it at least three times in recent memory. Each time, it's been like breaking out of jail." ...George Benson

GETTING OUT OF RUTS

Here's another creative malady that afflicts most guitarists at one time or another. The licks and moves that once seemed so new suddenly seem as fresh as some long-forgotten container of yogurt way in the back of the fridge. The trouble is you can't seem to play anything else. Don't despair. The perception that you're "in a rut" is generally a symptom that you are ready to move on to the next plateau. (The same goes for writer's block.) It's a tough rite of passage, but you're in excellent company.

"My favorite trick is not writing on the guitar all the time. If you write on guitar, you get into ruts. Whereas if you let your mind roam free, and then come back to the guitar and try and reproduce what's on your mind, you get a much broader scope. That's my excuse for not practicing very much. You have to live as well as play; that's what I think." ...Brian May

"I think of a guitar solo as an instant composition. You have a certain amount of time during which you're going to be making up a piece of music, and you hope the people who are working with you on stage are also interested in inventing music on the spot." ...Frank Zappa

THINK TRIBAL

Western culture is big on the idea of the brooding, solitary genius: Beethoven, Shakespeare, Einstein, Van Gogh, ...The modern cult of the guitar hero is just a subset of that: Beck, Clapton, Page, Van Halen, ...But music making is very often a collective activity, particularly in styles like rock and jazz that derive from African or other non-Western cultures. In many cases, the best inspiration doesn't come from inside you, or from some unseen cosmic force. It comes from the other musicians you're playing with. The best instrumentalists—both soloists and accompanists—are the ones that listen to the other players just as much as themselves. Maybe even more.

"It's funny, but I find out who I am when I'm stuck on the guitar. Because I say to myself, 'Oh no, what do I do here? I better just do what I did before.' If you're stuck, the only thing you can do is grab onto the nearest lifeline, which is usually something you've played before. But I'd rather try and be more spontaneous on stage." ...Jeff Beck

"Nine times out of ten, Keith [Richards] will have some riff and I'll know exactly how to sit in with it by some...magic. Keith and I call the way we play together 'an ancient form of weaving.'" ...Ron Wood

ALTERNATE TUNINGS

One sure-fire way of getting out of a rut is to change the tuning on your guitar. Suddenly, all those shopworn licks and tricks you learned in standard tuning will no longer work. It's like being dropped into some parallel universe. Scary but liberating. Your old habitual patterns of finger placement will produce different note combinations. These different note combinations will inspire new finger moves and chord shapes. Suddenly, you're approaching the guitar with the zeal of a novice. It's all new again. You've regained your innocence.

There is, after all, nothing sacred about so-called standard tuning. It's great for playing in keys like E and A, because the first and sixth strings can ring out open. But what if you're doing a song in D? Standard tuning is more than adequate, but guitarists often find it convenient to drop their low E string down to D when performing songs in keys like D and G. Fittingly enough, this is called **dropped D tuning**. From low string to high, these are the notes:

D–A–D–G–B–E

"The cool thing about open tunings is you just barre your finger behind a note and it changes the whole thing. You get into such weird transitions because you go from notes to notes you would never be able to go to in standard tuning." ...Stone Gossard

This tuning provides a low open-string tonic drone note when you play a D chord. Most standard chord shapes can easily be adapted to fit this small variation on standard tuning. And it's no big hassle to slip down into dropped D for a song or two in a set and then retune the low string back up to E. To venture a little further afield, you might try something called **double dropped D tuning**, in which the low and high E strings are both taken down a whole step:

D–A–D–G–B–D

Tunings other than standard have always existed. One very rich source of alternate tunings is folk music—an area where many of the originators had no access to, or no interest in, conventional guitar instruction. They just came up with their own tunings. One of the best-known tunings frequently used in folk music is:

D–A–D–G–A–D

In referring to this tuning, people generally just make the note names into two words and call it "**dad gad.**" It's what's known as a **modal tuning**. No two open strings form a third—the interval that tells the ear whether a chord is minor or major. So it's good tuning for drones and power chords. DADGAD is by no means the only modal tuning. Here are just a few other possibilities:

D–A–D–E–A–D	C–G–D–G–A–D	D–A–D–D–A–D
E–A–E–E–A–E	D–A–E–E–A–A	D–A–D–A–A–D

Note that the last four tunings contain two adjacent **unison** strings (i.e., they're tuned to the same note). This is very useful for playing passages that emulate the sound of a twelve-string guitar or a dulcimer.

"I had a problem with standard tuning. Somebody probably just put it on their instrument 300 years ago because the strings didn't break if they did it like that. E–A–D–G–B–E doesn't strike me as being a particularly intelligent tuning." ...Robert Fripp

Other tunings, particularly those favored by slide guitar players, include either major or minor thirds, to form a chord when all six strings are strummed open. Here are a few common **open chord tunings**:

D–A–D–F♯–A–D (D major)
C–G–C–G–C–E (C major)
E–A–C–E–A–E (A minor)
D–G–D–G–B–D (G major)
E–B–E–G–B–E (E minor)

Rock and roll guitarists, those archetypal mavericks, have always gravitated toward alternate tunings. Back in the sixties, Lou Reed invented what he called the **ostrich guitar**: all six strings tuned to the same note. He initially used it on a failed dance craze single called "The Ostrich" and later put it to more memorable use on the Velvet Underground classic "All Tomorrow's Parties." Rolling Stones guitarist Keith Richards has used several different opening tunings during the course of his career. But he's perhaps most closely identified with a variant on open G tuning (given above) in which he takes the low string off his guitar. You can play many Stones songs far more authentically once you know the five-string **"Keef tuning"**:

G–D–G–B–D

"Only five strings, three notes. In a way it's like the blues itself. The very fact that you're restricted to a few notes really makes you dig deep. And in fact, you can strike chords that you can't get on a six-string. If you hear guys playing 'Brown Sugar' on a six-string guitar, they're never gonna get it right. They get pretty close sometimes. But you're never gonna get that spatial ring going. 'Cause you've got too many notes to cover." ...Keith Richards

KEITH RICHARDS

© Michael Putland / Retna LTD.

"A new tuning triggers a different kind of logic." ...Thurston Moore

On the more cerebral side of rock, restlessly experimental guitarist Robert Fripp (King Crimson, League of Gentlemen, Sunday All Over the World) devised a tuning of his own, which became the basis of a whole method of teaching and playing that he calls Guitar Craft. Fripp's **Guitar Craft tuning** is a C major pentatonic affair, with fifths between all adjacent strings except the top two:

C–G–D–A–E–G

ALTERNATIVE ALTERNATES

Alternate tunings became popular among alternative rock guitarists in the late eighties and early nineties, when the Seattle grunge sound came to dominate the indie rock scene. But the groundwork had been laid earlier in the eighties by New York noise guitar pioneers **Sonic Youth**. Drawing on influences from rock and from avant garde guitar composers like Glenn Branca and Rys Chatham, Sonic Youth guitarists Lee Ranaldo and Thurston Moore took alternate tunings to new extremes. They were innovative in their use of unconventional string gauges and dissonant tunings, which included strings tuned to half steps and other cacophonous intervals. Moore and Ranaldo's guitars are often tuned completely differently for any given song. For example, on the songs "Dirty Boots" (from their breakthrough album *Goo*), "Chapel Hill," "Wish Fulfillment," and "Swimsuit Issue" (from *Dirty*, the follow-up to *Goo*), they're tuned as follows:

Moore: E–G–D–G–E–D (with second string lower than the third)
Ranaldo: E–E–B–B–E–F♯

For "Silver Rocket" (*Daydream Nation*) and "Theresa's Sound World" (*Dirty*), they use these tunings:
Moore: A–C–C–G–G♯–C
Ranaldo: A–A–E–E–A–A

Another Sonic Youth stalwart, the so-called "Kool Thing/Death Valley" tuning, is used on both guitars for *Dirty's* "100%" and "On the Strip":

F♯–F♯ (unison)–F♯–F♯ (unison, an octave higher)–E–B

Stone Gossard, guitarist with Seattle chartbusters **Pearl Jam**, is also a confirmed user of alternate tunings. He gravitates more toward conventional open tunings, such as dropped D (used on "Garden" from Pearl Jam's influential debut album *Ten*), open D (D–A–D–F♯–A–D) on "Even Flow" and "Oceans" from *Ten*, and a variant on open A (E–A–C♯–E–A–E) on "Deep" from the same album.

Soundgarden's hirsute lead guitarist Kim Thayil is another Seattlite with a penchant for alternate tunings. He drops his low E string all the way down to B (generally using a .056-gauge string), which is one factor in Soundgarden's heavier-than-kryptonite guitar sound. Other tunings used on Soundgarden's album *Badmotorfinger* include:

D–G–D–G–B–E ("New Damage")
D–A–D–G–B–B ("Face Pollution")

Another tuning ploy favored by Soundgarden, Metallica, Silverchair, and countless other heavy bands is to use standard tuning intervals but bring the whole thing down a whole step or minor third. In other words, instead of tuning all the strings relative to a low E, they'll tune everything to a low D or C♯:

D–G–C–F–A–D
C♯–F♯–B–E–G♯–C♯

COUNTRY AND BEYOND

At the other end of the spectrum, there is a variation on standard tuning known as **Nashville** (or "**high-strung**") **tuning**. The low E through G strings are replaced with lighter-gauge D through E strings and tuned up an octave higher than usual. (This amounts to the same thing as using just the "high" strings on a twelve-string guitar.) On acoustics or electrics, this produces a high, delicate, "angelic" tone. In recording, Nashville tuning is often used to double-track a strummed rhythm guitar part played in standard tuning, giving the part a shimmering high-end aura.

But many guitarists feel that the best approach to alternate tunings is to invent your own. Tunings can be devised to meet the demands of a specific composition, or just explored in a "close your eyes and turn the pegs" fashion. Many players, from Sonic Youth to Joni Mitchell, continually invent new tunings. They deliberately court the element of surprise. The exhilaration of the unknown—that moment when your old familiar guitar becomes a brand-new instrument—keeps them twirling their tuning pegs.

BILLY GIBBONS

© Jay Blakesberg / Petna LTD.

"The lowest ZZ Top can tune is probably close to D. Very close to where we live in Texas is a Santa Fe Railroad train on point. And if we're lucky, we can tune to the train horn. We've decided that's somewhere around D." ...Billy Gibbons

© John Atashian / Retna LTD.

ADRIAN BELEW

the creative guitarist

FUN WITH APPLIANCES

Anything from high drama to low comedy can be wrested from a guitar by "preparing" it. The idea comes from work done by avant garde composer John Cage starting in the late 1930s and early 1940s. Cage slipped metal bolts, paper clips, bits of rubber, paper, and felt under, over, and around the strings of a grand piano, causing it to emit a bumptious series of creaks, buzzes, thunks, and rattles that set serious Western classical music on its ear.

"A bobby pin on the neck of a guitar, in the right position, will immediately give you something between ring modulation and the sound of a steel drum." ...Adrian Belew

The same principles can be—and have been—applied to guitar. In a sense, slide guitar is a preparation. Early bluesmen would take the slender part of an ordinary glass bottle and slide it across the strings, over the fretboard. This allows for glissando effects not achievable with ordinary guitar playing technique, and also produces microtones outside of the Western tempered scale. Whoever did this first was being incredibly innovative. Who knew that, years later, it would become an instrument of unspeakable torture at sadistic gatherings known as "jam nites"?

Taking a cue from both Cage and Delta blues, the sixties guitar titans eagerly sought out wild ways to elicit brand-new tones from their instruments. Pete Townshend hit on the idea of scraping a mike stand, with an old-fashioned grooved clutch, across the guitar strings. Eddie Phillips of Creation took a violin bow to his guitar—a trick that was later adopted and popularized by Jimmy Page. Early Pink Floyd records are filled with like-minded experiments.

"On the middle section of 'Saucerful of Secrets,' most of the time the guitar was lying on the floor, and we took one of the legs unscrewed from a mike stand and were just whizzing it up and down the neck, not very subtly. Another technique—we did this a bit later on—is where you take a small piece of steel and rub it from side to side on the strings, so it's like bowing. And I just turned on the delay system until it was feeding back and the delays were regenerating more than the original signal." ...David Gilmour

One whole family of guitar preparations involves attaching foreign objects to the strings, and/or wedging them between the strings and the fretboard. Sonic Youth have been known to use screwdrivers for this purpose. Experimental guitar legend Fred Frith is fond of alligator clips. The world is full of ordinary household items that are secretly just dying to make music.

"I had a guitar once where the whole fretboard was covered with tin foil. That was a lot of fun because you would destroy it as you played. The tin foil would start to come off and the sound would keep changing. Wrapping pipe cleaners around the strings is good too. The little bit of metal in the pipe cleaner creates harmonics when you play the open strings. And you can move the pipe cleaners up and down when you're playing and get these nice scraping sounds." ...Eugene Chadbourne

Striking or strumming the strings with something other than your fingers or a pick constitutes another, often hilarious, set of guitar preparations. Eugene Chadbourne (a true guitar eccentric, who also invented the Electrified Garden Rake) discovered that rubbing a balloon up and down the guitar strings produces some rather interesting tones. David Bowie guitarist Reeves Gabrels employs a vibrator to excite his strings. Hard rock virtuoso Paul Gilbert has been known to play his axe with an electric drill. Three ordinary picks are attached to a small wooden dowel, which is then inserted into the chuck of the drill. The drill rotates the picks for a blurry, high-speed picking effect. Adrian Belew took barbecue tongs to his guitar when performing with Laurie Anderson (but opted for an ordinary pick for his work with Bowie, King Crimson, Talking Heads, and Nine Inch Nails). Speaking of King Crimson, bassist Tony Levin sometimes "drums" his strings with sawed-off drumsticks attached to his fingertips. Onstage, Mark Chung, bassist with German industrial pioneers Einstürzende Neubauten would perch atop a length of sewer pipe and scrape his bass strings along its curved concrete surface.

The best preparations have an element of performance value, as well as interesting sonic qualities. Raid the kitchen or the garage and try some of your own. Only do be careful of your guitar's finish.

ANGUS YOUNG

© Michael Putland / Retna LTD.

WHAT TO KNOW, WHAT TO DO, WHAT TO BRING

the performing guitarist

"I've had my pants fall off on stage, and was out there in my wedding tackle for all to see. I've even had my shorts stolen a couple of times." ...Angus Young, AC/DC

PERFORMING LIVE IS AN ADVENTURE, TO SAY THE LEAST. YOU SHOW WHAT YOU'VE GOT (MUSICALLY SPEAKING, THAT IS, UNLESS YOU'RE LIKE ANGUS), YOU DO IT IN REAL TIME, AND YOU GET AN INSTANT RESPONSE. WHEN THE RESPONSE IS GOOD, IT'S ONE OF THE GREATEST PLEASURES A MUSICIAN CAN EXPERIENCE. AND, WITH A LITTLE PREPARATION, YOU CAN REDUCE THE RISK OF GETTING CAUGHT WITH YOUR PANTS DOWN.

BUILDING A LIVE GUITAR RIG

Simplicity is a major virtue when putting together a live guitar setup. Gigging and touring are a lot like war—your equipment should have all the qualities of good weaponry:

1. highly portable
2. quick and easy to set up and tear down
3. very sturdily built
4. as few "moving parts" as possible
5. fairly impervious to dirt, mud, heat, cold, spit, beer, blood, etc.

Avoid the elaborate and the arcane when assembling a rig for gigging. Remember that many nuances and sonic subtleties are lost when you're playing live. It's not like recording. No one in the audience will be listening on headphones. (Given the room acoustics and ambient noise levels in your average rock club, they probably *should* be wearing headphones, but that's another issue.) So maybe you should leave that delicate, vintage sixties tape echo unit at home. Even the most discerning audience member will be unable to hear any difference between it and the "Trippin' Echo" preset on a $300 multi-effects device. Besides, things like vintage tape echo units have a funny way of getting stolen at gigs.

So, the simpler the better. An amp. One rack mount multi-effect device, or a few stomp boxes. Remember that for each piece of equipment you add, you're increasing the grief factor. Another cord to crap out. Another battery to change. Also, your rig should allow you to switch sounds very quickly and easily. Avoid setups where you have to fiddle with a lot of different knobs or—perish the thought—repatch anything.

Solid-state amps are much more roadworthy—lighter and less fragile—than their tube counterparts. If you gig with a tube amp, it should be because

The Hair Dryer Trick

Tube amps require special attention in cold climates. If your amp has been out in the cold for a long time, you shouldn't turn it on as soon as you bring it indoors. This could damage the tubes. Instead, wait for the tubes to reach room temperature before switching the amp on.

Life on the road, however, doesn't always allow cozy little intervals in which your tubes can reach the ideal serving temperature for vintage claret. For instance, you may have to do a soundcheck, or show, as soon as you arrive at the venue. What to do?

Here is yet another use for that wonderful household beauty apparatus, the hair dryer. Fire up the dryer and blow gently on tubes to help them warm up a little quicker than they would naturally. But be sure to **hold the dryer a good foot or more away from the tubes.** Putting the thing right up against the tubes and blasting away is even worse than turning the amp on as soon as it's been brought inside. The tubes still need to warm up gradually if the glass isn't going to crack. A hair dryer should only be used to accelerate this natural process slightly.

that's absolutely the only way you can get the tone you need. Yes, some "workingman's brand" solid-state amp looks far less cool than a tweaked-out vintage tube amp that's like something out of a "Man from U.N.C.L.E." episode. But most pros would agree that it's not such a good idea to bring a rare old vintage amp out on a club tour.

All amps, ideally, should have their own flight cases when they go out on the road. Good strong casters (wheels) on the flight cases will help you save your energy for the show and also reduce the possibility that you'll drop the amp while attempting to carry it. Stomp boxes, luckily, can travel in a nice cheap suitcase. If you can't afford a flight case for your rack mount gear, save the box and Styrofoam packing material it came in. It's much better to use those than to throw the thing into the back of the van without any protection.

"I was traveling in Africa in a station wagon with my Strat strapped to the top. The driver was going about 90 mph, and my guitar blew off the top of the station wagon, popped out of the case, and was bouncing down the street. The driver stopped, and I ran out to keep him from running over my guitar as he was backing up. I picked up that Strat, and the E string was out of tune. One tuning machine got hit, but it wasn't broken. Just bent. I said to that guitar: 'You lived through that? You'll be my favorite guitar for the rest of my life.' " ...Buddy Guy

Single-coil pickups present another prickly issue for the performing guitarist. They tend to produce a lot more hum than any other kind of pickup. While this might be barely noticeable at home, the hum can get very intense under stage lighting. There's not too much you can do about this. The electromagnetic properties that make single coil pickups sound the wonderful way they do are the very same properties that make them hum. So if you love the sound of single coils, you have to live with the buzz. A slight reduction of hum can be achieved by using good shielded cable and shielding the inside of the pickup compartments with copper tape or silver paint. But the best bet is to use a noise suppressor: a device that will automatically cut the volume, and therefore the hum, when you're not playing. And when you are playing, the signal will mask the hum. Replacing single coil pickups with stacked humbucking pickups (which fit into a single coil slot) will get rid of the hum, but will also change the sound. Ditto for switching to active pickups.

Wireless systems give guitarists maximum onstage mobility. Without a patch cord to shackle you to your amp, you can go anywhere. But, while wireless technology has gotten very sophisticated in the years it's been around, many guitarists still feel that it "colors" or "pinches" their tone. Also, wireless systems continue to be vulnerable to interference from local radio waves, CB radio, and all kinds of other unseen forces that go with modern civilization. So it's a good idea to have a patch cord as a backup.

Speaking of backups, the big-time pros carry spares of *everything*—guitars, amps, effects, and accessories. This isn't a financial possibility for most working guitarists or casual gigsters. However, if at all possible, you should have a spare guitar with you when you play a show. Even if it's the incredibly cheap, embarrassing one you got for your tenth birthday. If you break a string on stage, a spare guitar will enable you to finish out a song or a set—especially if you don't have a guitar roadie. And of course, you should at least have two full sets of spare strings and extra picks.

HOW MUCH WATTAGE IS ENOUGH?

The archetypal image of the rock guitarist—flanked by a wall of 100-watt Marshall stacks—dates from the late sixties, when PA systems were very primitive and bands had to rely on their own amplification to fill a hall. Today, even modest-sized rock clubs are generally equipped with bruisingly powerful P.A. systems. The guitarist's amp is miked and the PA system does the work of filling the hall. The guitar amp's only jobs are to create a good tone and enough volume to be heard on stage. (And with today's sophisticated monitor mixes, part of the latter task can be performed by the monitor system.)

For blues, jazz, country, reggae, funk, R&B, and more Beatlesque forms of rock, 20–30-watt combo amps generally do the trick, enabling guitarists to achieve a nice balance with a drum kit. And even for the loudest, heaviest rock styles, a 50-watt amp is all you need to play a club, theatre, or even an arena. Guitar players who rely on amp distortion should bear in mind that a 50-watt amp will go into distortion more readily (i.e., at a lower volume) than a 100-watt amp. Excessive amounts of onstage volume make it difficult for the sound mixer to get a well balanced sound in the house PA. (And since this is the sound the audience hears, it should be the first consideration.) Over-loud guitar amps on stage also make it hard to get a good monitor mix. Vocalists have trouble hearing, and the monitor speakers start feeding back. Also, excessively high onstage volume levels will damage your hearing, not to mention that of other band members and the punters right in front of the stage.

STEVE JONES

© Steve Eichner / Retna LTD.

It's all a matter of scale. A 50-watt amp going into distortion on a smallish club stage is just as cataclysmic an event as a 100- or 200-watt amp going into distortion on a gigantic stage in some vast sports arena. Also remember that the PA system acts as an aural magnifying glass. Even a little 10-watt amp can be made to loom large in the house mix and overpower a twenty-piece drum kit and side-of-beef bass rig—kind of like those sci-fi movies where a little 10-inch rubber monster is made to look like a giant towering over a city.

Of course, there are those who will argue—and rightly so—that a 100-watt amp going into distortion has different tonal qualities than a 50-watt going into distortion. However, the advantages of keeping stage volumes at a manageable level far outweigh the subtle differences in tone you can get from using a 100-watt amp in a club.

One last point: When you see a guitarist flanked by ten or twenty amp stacks at a heavy metal show, bear in mind that only one or two of those amps and stacks are actually switched on and putting out sound. The others are there purely for visual impact—the rubber monster effect in reverse.

"You do not need a huge wall of amps behind you on any stage, ever. You wanna hear yourself, you just need four bloody little monitors on a fifty-foot stage. That's fine. Just so long as they work. If they don't work, then you've got real problems." ...Steve Jones, Sex Pistols

ANATOMY OF A GIG

For every hour a band spends on stage, there are many hours of preparation and work to be completed. Artists signed to a record label, or who generate a large income from playing live, have people to take care of most day-of-show preparations for them. Aspiring and semi-pro bands, unfortunately, have to do most of the work themselves. Playing a gig is typically a ten- to twelve-hour work day, from the time you leave your house or rehearsal space to the time you get back home. (Solo acoustic guitarists have it a bit easier.) So learn how to pace yourself.

BEFORE THE DAY OF THE SHOW

Someone should phone the venue and confirm what time soundcheck is. If you're unfamiliar with the venue, find out where the load-in entrance is located. If you are knowledgeable about sound reinforcement equipment (or have your own sound mixer), you can also "advance the PA"—i.e., talk to the house sound mixer and scope out the house system. This will give you some idea of what to expect and alert you to any supplemental equipment of your own you might need to bring (monitors, microphones, etc.). However, if you don't have anyone in your camp who really knows PA gear, don't try to do this. You'll probably just irritate the house sound person, which is definitely not a good thing to do.

DAVE NAVARRO

© John Popplewell / Retna LTD.

THE DAY OF THE SHOW

1. **Eat a good lunch.** If soundcheck runs late or there's a problem, you may not get a chance to eat dinner. Also, many musicians don't like to eat a big meal too soon before they go on stage. It's not much fun feeling "bloated" when you're all keyed up to play. But it's just as unpleasant to have hunger pangs because you haven't eaten anything in twelve hours. So, at lunchtime, load up on protein, nutrients, and all that other good stuff mom says you need. And it never hurts to carry some "squirrel food" (trail mix, nuts, raisins, etc.) in case you get hungry at the venue. You'll make friends, too!

2. **Load the van.** The heavy, bulky things (like speaker cabinets) go on the bottom and toward the center of the vehicle. Grille cloths should be placed face down, or two of them face-to-face, so that a mike stand or other pointy stick won't poke through the grille and take out a speaker cone. Position lighter, more delicate stuff on top of and around the speaker cabinets, distributing all weight evenly. Try to make the load "flat," so that gear doesn't fly around when the driver hits the brakes. Rope and/or bungee cords can be used to secure objects.

   Allow about an hour to pack the van. (More if you're dealing with elevators, stairs, a "long carry" or more equipment than the average five-piece rock band usually hauls.) Figure out how much time it will take to drive to the venue, then allow yourself twice that amount of time. This will cover you in the event of breakdowns, getting lost, and having to turn back halfway there when the drummer suddenly realizes he's forgotten his kick drum pedal.

3. **Load-in.** The gear is taken off the van and brought into the venue, where it's generally stacked somewhere alongside the stage, preparatory to being set up on stage for soundcheck. Someone at the venue will generally tell you where to stack the stuff. At higher-end places there'll be a stage manager (presumably) organizing the whole thing. Otherwise, the sound mixer might be in charge. Or you may get there ahead of anybody who knows anything, so you'll have to use your common sense.
4. **Soundcheck.** Soundcheck etiquette is fairly clear-cut. Acts soundcheck in opposite order of the show sequence. That is, the headliner (the act that goes on last) soundchecks first. And the first act to go on soundchecks last. It's done this way for two reasons. For one, in deference to their star status, the headliners are given first crack at soundchecking and thus the maximum available time in which to iron out any problems that arise. The second reason has to do with how the equipment is managed onstage. After one band finishes playing, their equipment is pulled to the side, and the next act's gear is waiting right behind.

   A finer point of soundcheck etiquette is that you're not supposed to dawdle when you're up there. It's not a time to jam or rehearse or write a new song. You do what must be done as quickly as possible and leave the stage, so the next act can have their turn. But sometimes legitimate problems arise that take a long time to sort out. So if things are running late and the doors are just about to open, the opening band might not get a chance to do a soundcheck. If this happens to you, don't throw a tantrum. It's not a personal attack. It happens all the time. A good sound mixer will be able to get a decent mix together over the course of your first song or two. That's when the club is usually just filling up anyway.

So what's supposed to happen during a soundcheck? You set all your gear up, turn it on, and listen for any grounding problems (hums and buzzes) that need to be corrected. After dealing with this, the sound mixer, or his/her assistant, places microphones and hooks up direct boxes on instruments like keyboards and (sometimes) bass. The sound mixer then generally asks to hear one instrument at a time. The drums usually take the most time to get sounding good without any feedback. So be patient. When your turn comes, give the sound mixer an idea of the loudest and the softest you're going to play: full screaming distortion, clean sounds, the range of effects you'll be using, the brightest, most trebly sounds you'll be using, and the woofiest low tones you've got.

As a guitarist, your jobs during soundcheck are: (1) to make sure all your gear is in proper working order after its ride in the van, and (2) to position yourself and your equipment in the best possible spot so that you can hear your instrument and everyone else in the band, and so that you can get what you need out of your amp. (Another good reason for getting a flight case for a combo amp is that you can place the amp on top of the case, where the speakers are more or less on the same plane with the guitar's pickups, enabling better control of things like sustain and feedback.)

The sound mixer's jobs are to get a good house mix on the band and to set up a monitor mix that everyone on stage is comfortable with. At better venues, there will be a separate person to mix the monitors and a separate monitor mix board off to the side of the stage. Bands can sometimes bring their own monitor system into a venue. If possible, it's good to use your own monitor mixer and house mixer—people who know your sound and your requirements. Just bear in mind that the house sound people are the ones in charge. Your sound mixer knows your music, but the house person knows the room and the rig.

Hopefully.

In your travels, you will encounter everything from highly skilled sound engineers to guys with steel plates in their heads who run the mixing board

"I work out seriously before each show: pushups, situps, stretching, yoga—for an hour straight. I usually eat at about 10 or 11 in the morning, and then I don't eat again until after the gig. I drink about four bottles of ginseng. I never do shows high. There's too much going on." ...Jesse Tobias, guitarist with Alanis Morissette

while also tending bar. Part of the musician's freewheeling gypsy lifestyle is learning how to deal with the bizarre cast of characters found behind mixing boards. If you seem professional and organized, the house sound person will be more inclined to trust you and let you do things your way. Providing data like stage plots and microphone charts generally creates a good impression. Then again, there are people who just get mad when shown pieces of paper with writing on them. In such cases, all you can do is smile and hope for the best.

5. **Pre-show.** Stay cool but keep your guitars at room temperature. The time between soundcheck and showtime can hang heavy on your hands. The basic goal here is to spend the time in a way that conserves your energy and keeps you fairly calm. You'll get enough of an adrenaline rush when you hit the stage. You don't want to get all wound up (psychologically or chemically) before hand. Musicians spend their preshow time in all kinds of ways. Some do yoga and meditate. Some read. Some play chess. Some just hang out and talk. Drawing up the set list is generally a great time-killer. Bands with elaborate stage costumes and makeup spend most of the time primping. Some musicians like to go out front and watch the other acts. Others hate to watch the other acts and like to get out of the venue entirely. But you should only do this if you've got someone to keep an eye on the gear so nothing gets stolen.

   Remember to take care of your guitar as well as yourself. If possible, keep the guitars on the stage while you're waiting to go on. Backstage areas tend to be much colder than it is on stage. The difference in temperature can create tuning problems.

6. **Showtime.** All the work and grief endured up to this point have been so that you can enjoy this moment. Make the most of it.

7. **Post-show.** Don't look so smug. You still gotta get paid and get the gear out of the venue. In payment schemes that involve a percentage of the "door," you'll have to wait till the last band is finished before you can settle up with your good friend the club owner. Even if you can get your gear out of the venue while the other bands are still playing, resist the temptation to load up the van before getting paid (so as to get home a little quicker). While you're inside collecting the evening's rewards, someone else might not be able to resist the temptation to pop the lock on your van and collect your gear.

   If you keep your wits about you till the very end, you'll feel like a real road warrior as the van speeds off into the night.

"I don't even know the audience is there. It's nice if they are. But I'm paying attention to the instrument." ...Frank Zappa

What to Bring: A Checklist of Useful Items

1. Flashlight. Indispensable for last-minute repairs on darkened stages, or just getting on and off pitch-black stages without breaking your neck. Also handy backstage, where the lighting is often less than ideal. And when the van breaks down in the middle of the night, you'll understand why this is the one implement you should never leave home without. The flashlight industry makes some sporty, compact models with a hole for a chain in the base. So you can wear your flashlight around your neck, or hang it from your belt, or a pierced body appendage. You're less likely to lose it this way, and when you need it, it'll be somewhere about your person.

2. Ground lifters. Those little rubber adapters that convert a three-pronged AC cord into a two-pronger. And the house sound person never seems to have enough to go around.

CAUTION: Ground lifters should only be used at venues that have only two-prong wall sockets, and the wire or tab on the front of the adapter should always be connected to ground (the screw that holds the outlet face plate on is usually grounded). Using them to lift ground on a three-prong cord creates a risk of electric shock. The correct way to lift a hum-inducing ground is to use a direct box with a switch that lifts the signal ground, rather than the power ground.

3. Duct tape. In an imperfect universe, we're lucky we've got duct tape. It's good for everything from attaching spare picks to a mike stand to tacking down wires on stage so you won't trip over them to sealing off hotel room doors so smoke won't get in (or out).

4. Guitar tuner. The difference between a crappy set and a good one. It's best to keep your tuner "in line" so you can kill your amp volume and check tuning during a set. Some modern amps even provide a separate tuner jack for doing this. Remember to bring two extra patch cords for your tuner.

5. Spares. Extra fuses for all amps, spare strings, picks, and a spare guitar strap. Ideally, you should have two of anything and everything you absolutely need to do a show.

6. Tools. Think Murphy's Law. At the very least, you should bring along the following:

a. A flat-head and a Phillips head (star) screwdriver.

b. A set of hex (Allen) and/or socket wrenches that includes all sizes needed to adjust the bridge, tremolo system, and everything else on your guitar(s).

c. Needle-nose pliers (the kind with a built-in wire cutter, for trimming new guitar strings after you've put them on).

A few different companies make "all in one" guitar tools that combine many of the above functions. A good old boy scout/girl scout/Swiss Army pocket knife is never an unwelcome companion on the road. If you're a real "Tool Time" type, you might want to bring a soldering iron, solder, a wire stripper, and (for longer tours) an oscilloscope.

7. Ear plugs. Prolonged exposure to rock and roll volume levels will damage your hearing. Upper midrange frequencies (about 800 Hz and up) are the first to go. Not only will this impair your ability to hear crucial frequencies in your own music and that of others, but you'll also be unable to hear things like women's voices in a room where other people are talking. Next comes tinnitus—a continual ringing in the ears that never goes away.

The way to prevent all this is to wear ear plugs at every gig (whether you're performing or in the audience). Foam plugs are the cheapest and most effective. Many musicians, however, feel that these block out too much high-frequency information. An alternative, if the volume levels aren't ear-splitting, is to wear special, vented "musicians" or "swimmers" ear plugs. These let in more high frequencies. If you're very particular about protecting your ears and hearing a full, musical frequency spectrum, there are several companies that will custom-make ear plugs to fit your ears.

8. Pen and paper. For writing out set lists, lyrics, and chord charts, jotting down important phone numbers, signing autographs,...

9. Corkscrew / bottle opener / can opener. Essential for imported beers, wine, sundry groceries. 'Cause there's more to life than Bud and Miller.

10. Work gloves. Get the kind with rubber handgrips. They enable you to get a firm grasp on amps and other heavy items, so you can protect your hands while loading and unloading the van. Will also keep your hands warm in chilly backstage areas.

the well-read guitarist

For further reading, here are some recommended titles that are distributed by Hal Leonard.

Amps! The Other Half Of Rock n' Roll
(HL00330057)

Basic Guitar
(HL00183051)

Dictionary Of Guitar Styles
(HL00695162)

Fast Track Music Instruction Guitar 1
(HL00697282)

Fast Track Series Chords and Scales For Guitar
(HL00697291)

Getting Great Guitar Sounds
(HL00330375)

Guitar FX Cookbook
(HL00695080)

Hal Leonard Beginning Guitar Super Book
(HL00697207)

Legends Of Rock Guitar Fake Book 2nd Edition
(HL00240023)

The Complete Guide to Guitar and Amp Maintenance
(HL00330117)

The Hal Leonard Real Jazz Book
(HL00240097)

The Ultimate Fake Book 2nd Edition
(HL00240024)

The Ultimate Guitar Chord User's Guide
(HL00697231)

The Ultimate Pop Rock Fake Book 3rd Edition
(HL00240099)

Wolf Marshall Guitar Method Basics 1 w/CD
(HL00697221)

about the author

Over the course of his eighteen-year career, Alan di Perna's work has been published in Billboard, Creem, Guitar Player, Guitar World, Keyboard, Mix, Musician, Raygun, and Rolling Stone, among other magazines. One of America's most respected music journalists, he is currently West Coast Editor of Guitar World. His previous book for Hal Leonard was Fender Classic Moments.